The Lens of Love

The Lens of Love

A closer look at the Book of Job
and Paul's Thorn in the Flesh

Susan C. Hall

Copyright © 2025 Susan C. Hall
All Rights Reserved
ISBN: 979-83-11639-10-1

Scriptures marked NKJV are taken from the NEW KING JAMES VERSION (NKJV): Scripture taken from the NEW KING JAMES VERSION®. Copyright© 1982 by Thomas Nelson, Inc. Used by permission. All rights reserved.

Scriptures marked YLT are taken from the YOUNG'S LITERAL TRANSLATION (YLT): Scripture quotations marked (YLT) are taken from the 1898 YOUNG'S LITERAL TRANSLATION OF THE HOLY BIBLE by J.N. Young, (Author of the Young's Analytical Concordance), public domain.

Scriptures marked NIV are taken from the NEW INTERNATIONAL VERSION (NIV): Scripture taken from THE HOLY BIBLE, NEW INTERNATIONAL VERSION ®. Copyright© 1973, 1978, 1984, 2011 by Biblica, Inc.™. Used by permission of Zondervan

Scriptures marked RSV are taken from the REVISED STANDARD VERSION (RSV): Scripture taken from the REVISED STANDARD VERSION, Grand Rapids: Zondervan, 1971.

Scriptures marked AMP are taken from the AMPLIFIED BIBLE (AMP): Scripture taken from the AMPLIFIED® BIBLE, Copyright © 1954, 1958, 1962, 1964, 1965, 1987 by the Lockman Foundation Used by Permission. (www.Lockman.org)

Scripture quotations marked (NLT) are taken from the *HOLY BIBLE*, NEW LIVING TRANSLATION, copyright ©1996, 2004, 2015 by Tyndale House Foundation. Used by permission of Tyndale House Publishers, Carol Stream, Illinois 60188. All rights reserved.

Scriptures marked (NASB) are taken from The NEW AMERICAN STANDARD BIBLE (NASB): Scripture quotations taken from the (NASB®) NEW AMERICAN STANDARD BIBLE®, Copyright © 1960, 1971, 1977, 1995, 2020 by The Lockman Foundation. Used by permission. All rights reserved. lockman.org

Scripture quotations from The Authorized (King James) Version marked (KJV). Rights in the Authorized Version in the United Kingdom are vested in the Crown. Reproduced by permission of the Crown's patentee, Cambridge University Press.

Front Cover Artwork created using Canva and an AI generated image via canva.com 2025

Back cover photo credit: Tamerra Moir

To my Heavenly Father who is Love.

To my family who have been models, examples and teachers of love, who have inspired love and whom I deeply love.

TABLE OF CONTENTS

INTRODUCTION 1

CHAPTER ONE - A STUDY OF THE BOOK OF JOB 4
    The Journey Begins 4
    What do we know about Job? 5
    Behind the Scenes 8
    Why did God mention Job in the first place? 10
    The Request 11
    What happened to Job's hedge of protection? 12
    What does God use to teach His people? 15
    What does Satan attack? 17
    What was Satan's intention wtih these attacks? 18
    What was Job's response? 19

CHAPTER TWO - JOB CHAPTER 2 23
    Another Peek Behind the Scenes 23
    The Enemy's Response 25
    Job's Response 2.0 26
    The Wife 26
    Job's Friends 27
    What was Job's friends' reaction? 28
    Getting to know Job's friends 28

CHAPTER THREE - JOB CHAPTER 3 31
    What was Job thinking? 31
    The Fear 32

CHAPTER FOUR - JOB CHAPTER 4 36
    Eliphaz Speaks – Experience/Self-Effort 36
    Dream or Nightmare? 38

CHAPTER FIVE - JOB CHAPTER 5 40
    Experience Speaks 40
    A Closer Look 41

CHAPTER SIX - JOB CHAPTER 6 42
    And the award goes to… 42
    The Ransom 43
    Where is the Spot on the Spotless Record? 43
    Hopelessness 44
    The Blame Game 45

CHAPTER SEVEN - JOB CHAPTER 7 46
Is there any hope? 46
You're being watched! 47
What have I done? 47

CHAPTER EIGHT - JOB CHAPTER 8 49
Bildad – Justice 49
Bildad – Tradition 50
Justice in Action 51

CHAPTER NINE - JOB CHAPTER 9 53
What's the use? 53
A Direct Line 54
A Reason for Hope 54

CHAPTER TEN - JOB CHAPTER 10 56
Puzzled 56
Back in Court 57

CHAPTER ELEVEN - JOB CHAPTER 11 59
Zophar – Legalism 59
Measuring Up 60
To-Do List 60

CHAPTER TWELVE - JOB CHAPTERS 12 – 14 62
Foundations 62
Wisdom Explored 63
Purity 65

CHAPTER THIRTEEN - JOB CHAPTER 15 67
Eliphaz – Take Two 67
Eliphaz' Equation 68

CHAPTER FOURTEEN - JOB CHAPTERS 16 AND 17 69
Where is your focus? 71

CHAPTER FIFTEEN - JOB CHAPTERS 18 AND 19 73
Bildad – No mercy 73
See or be seen 74
The Big IF 74
Relationships attacked 75
Hope 76

CHAPTER SIXTEEN - JOB CHAPTERS 20 AND 21 78
Zophar – Ruffled Feathers 78
Job Unconvinced 79

CHAPTER SEVENTEEN - JOB CHAPTER 22 82
  The Golden Checklist 82

CHAPTER EIGHTEEN - JOB CHAPTER 23 86
  Unwavering 86
  Knowing in part 87

CHAPTER NINETEEN - JOB CHAPTER 24 88
  Hearing Job's heart 88

CHAPTER TWENTY - JOB CHAPTER 25 90
  The Voice of Judgement 90

CHAPTER TWENTY-ONE - JOB CHAPTER 26 93
  Sarcasm anyone? 93
  God's Greatness 94

CHAPTER TWENTY-TWO - JOB CHAPTER 27 95
  Forsaken? 95
  Choices 96
  Knowing that you know that you know 97

CHAPTER TWENTY-THREE - JOB CHAPTER 28 99
  In search of wealth 99
  In search of wisdom 100

CHAPTER TWENTY-FOUR - JOB CHAPTER 29 102
  Memory Lane 102
  Addressing Eliphaz' Accusations 104
  Respected to rejected 105

CHAPTER TWENTY-FIVE - JOB CHAPTER 30 107
  Perspective 107
  Case of Welfare 108
  Unseen evidence 108

CHAPTER TWENTY-SIX - JOB CHAPTER 31 110
  Five Stages 110
  Step Tracker 111
  Job rests his case 112

CHAPTER TWENTY-SEVEN - JOB CHAPTER 32 113
  Elihu 113
  Grace revealed 114
  Ready to burst 118

CHAPTER TWENTY-EIGHT - JOB CHAPTER 33 120
- Elihu Continues 120
- Depiction 121
- Food for thought 122
- Flesh and Bone 123
- In need of a Mediator and Ransom 123

CHAPTER TWENTY-NINE - JOB CHAPTER 34 127
- Evidence examined 127

CHAPTER THIRTY - JOB CHAPTER 35 129
- Questions of Righteousness 129
- Unchanging 130
- Unchanging Love 131

CHAPTER THIRTY-ONE - JOB CHAPTER 36 132
- Speaking on God's behalf 132
- Choices 133
- Warnings 134
- Comparing Psalm 107 135

CHAPTER THIRTY-TWO - JOB CHAPTER 37 137
- Thunder and Lightning 137
- The Rain 139
- Rest 139
- Clouds 140
- Stop and Consider 140

CHAPTER THIRTY-THREE - JOB CHAPTER 38 142
- Right in the midst 142
- Gird up your loins 144
- Comparing Résumés 144
- Q & A 145
- No Contest 146

CHAPTER THIRTY-FOUR - JOB CHAPTER 39 147
- God cares 147
- Strengths 148

CHAPTER THIRTY-FIVE - JOB CHAPTER 40 149
- A Change of Perspective 150
- Truth 150
- Payback 152
- Requirements 152
- Behemoth 153

CHAPTER THIRTY-SIX - **JOB CHAPTER 41** **155**
   LEVIATHAN 155

CHAPTER THIRTY-SEVEN - **JOB CHAPTER 42** **157**
   REVEALED 157
   EYE OPENING EXPERIENCE 159
   REVELATION 159
   A CLEAN SLATE 160
   ABOUT THE SACRIFICE 162
   RESTORATION 163
   THE VISITORS 163
   SEEING DOUBLE 164

CHAPTER THIRTY-EIGHT - **THE THORN IN THE FLESH** **168**
   WHAT IS THE THORN IN THE FLESH? 170
   WHO SENT THE THORN? 171
   WHY WAS THE THORN SENT? 171
   WHAT WAS PAUL'S RESPONSE? 173
   WHAT WAS GOD'S RESPONSE? 173
   A CLOSER LOOK AT PAUL 174
   WHAT WERE THE RESULTS? 177
   WHAT COULD THIS THORN REALLY HAVE BEEN? 178
   WHAT ABOUT HUMILITY? 180

CHAPTER THIRTY-NINE - **COMPARISONS BETWEEN JOB AND PAUL** **181**
   RELATIONSHIP WITH GOD 181
   UNDER ENEMY ATTACK 182
   CALLING OUT TO GOD 183
   A REFUGE AND A PLAN 183
   EQUIPPED 184
   VICTORY 184

CHAPTER FORTY - **RELEVANCE FOR TODAY** **185**
   WHOSE REPORT TO BELIEVE 185
   SOME EXAMPLES 186

CHAPTER FORTY-ONE - **IS YOUR LENS IN FOCUS? CHALLENGE** **188**

SCRIPTURES **191**

PRAYERS...**193**

INTRODUCTION

When I was a young child, I can remember asking my mom questions; lots of questions. Usually, these questions would conveniently come right at bedtime. The tradition has been passed down, it seems, as my daughters often come up with their most profound questions, too, at bedtime. I must have been around four years old when I asked my mom, "Who made God?" It is often hard for adults to wrap their head around the answer let alone a young child. My mother made many attempts to answer in an age appropriate way. She told me that God was not created; He is the Creator. She also said that it is hard for us, having been created, to understand God not being created. There were many efforts to bring me to understanding the concept of "eternal." However, in the end, my mom simply said, "I guess you'll just have to ask God when you see Him." At that very moment, I can remember picturing myself crawling up on God's lap and asking him a multitude of questions. There was no sense of "I'm not worthy!" or "God doesn't have time for me." I knew that I was a child of God and knew that I had the right to "come boldly to the throne of Grace" (Heb. 4:16 New King James Version).

I was very blessed to be raised in a family with not only a very loving father but also a very loving grandfather. I would spend a lot of time on their laps asking them questions and talking about just about anything. It really was not a stretch for me to think of God, my Heavenly Father, in the same way. I could relate the love I saw from my earthly father and grandfather to the love of God. Additionally, my grandfather was a minister. Each week at church, he would sit down with all of the children before they went to Sunday school. He would tell a little story or teach a Biblical principle. Because he was my grandpa, I would always wiggle my way into the spot right next to him. I never stopped anyone else from sitting there. I just made it my mission to sit there. In my mind, it was my spot. My grandpa never prevented me from boldly coming up to him. There was no reason for me to think God would.

As I grew, I started to hear people attribute unloving qualities to God. Usually, it would be in the name of God's sovereignty or God's infinite wisdom. People were almost eager to believe these unloving characteristics were God's out of His great love. This just didn't and still doesn't make much sense to me. So, here is my challenge: Whenever you read or hear something about God, whether in the Bible itself or from the pulpit or elsewhere, look at it through the lens of GOD IS LOVE.

Introduction

We know that on the basis of two or three witnesses, something can be established (2 Cor. 13:1, Deut. 19:15). Therefore, let us establish that God is love. Both First John 4:8 and First John 4:16 say word for word that God is love. If one would desire a Biblical definition of 'love' all they need to do is turn to First Corinthians 13 to find out that love is patient, kind and so forth. For me, it is easy to conclude that God, since He is love, is also the fullness of the characteristics listed in First Corinthians 13.

There are two main arguments people often use in order to defend their position of God doing unloving acts or "allowing" horrible things to happen in the lives of His creation. One is the sufferings of Job and the other is Paul's thorn in the flesh. I endeavor to address both in the following chapters. My hope is that, if we can get a full understanding of these instances, people will have no more barriers to wholly resting in the fullness of God's LOVE.

Chapter One

A STUDY OF THE BOOK OF JOB

THE JOURNEY BEGINS

For many years, I held the stance that people's teachings about Job's sufferings and Paul's thorn in the flesh were largely flawed. I always believed that God Almighty is loving and merciful. Over time, I encountered many people who would want to debate these beliefs. For example, they insisted that God would use sickness and trials to teach His people.

In the matter of Job, I was one who would usually read the beginning chapters and the final chapters of the Book of Job. I would often skip over the middle chapters as I did not fully understand them. The "comforters" have a lot to say throughout those middle chapters. Some of what they had to say seemed true while other things did not "sit right" with me. I did not know whether to trust their opinions or not.

There came a point, however, where I wanted to settle within myself once and for all whether what I believed to be true about Job and Paul was correct or whether the debaters were right all along. I determined to study both the Book of Job and the books in the Bible written by or about Paul chronologically up to and including Paul's thorn in the flesh. I did my best to set aside any biases and I resolved not to reference any commentaries or opinions written by others until my study was complete. Using a concordance, I searched out the meanings of the original Hebrew and Greek words used in the scriptures. Whenever I "got stuck" and did not understand a certain passage of scripture, I camped there, prayed and waited until Holy Spirit brought understanding and revelation.

It was a very exciting journey for me. There were days when one word would yield pages of revelation. It became clear at some point in the process, that a book was being formed. The message woven throughout both Biblical accounts needed to be shared. What follows is the fruit of my quest. It is my hope that it will be a blessing to many.

WHAT DO WE KNOW ABOUT JOB?

Scholars believe that the Book of Job is one of the oldest books in the Bible. Many figure that Job lived just after Abraham and overlapped the time of Moses. Genesis 46:13 mentions Job as being one of the sons of Issachar. If this were the same person, it would fit the timeline. It is even thought that Moses penned the Book of Job after having heard Job's firsthand account[1].

Job's name in the Hebrew can be translated as "hated" in the sense of "persecuted."[2] In Job 1:1 and Job 1:8, Job is described as being blameless, upright, fearing God and shunning evil. Looking through *Strong's Exhaustive Concordance of the Bible*, at the original Hebrew, it breaks down the meanings of each of these characteristics to give us a fuller picture. Following, is the breakdown:

> "Blameless" = Hebrew word *tām* = perfect, complete – one who lacks nothing in physical strength, beauty, etc.
> = sound, wholesome – an ordinary, quiet sort of person
> = complete, morally innocent, having integrity – one who is morally and ethically pure[3]
>
> *Gesenius' Hebrew-Chaldee Lexicon* defines *tām* as "whole, upright, always in a moral sense."[4]
>
> "Upright" = Hebrew word *yāšār* = straight, upright, correct, right[5]
>
> "Fearing" = Hebrew word *yārē'* = to fear, revere, be afraid[6]

The first time a specific word is used in the Bible can often give a deeper insight into the meaning of the word. It is often known as "First Mention" and can be a tool used by people who desire to dig deeper into the Word. The first use of the Hebrew word *yārē'* was in Genesis 3:10 when God, in the garden after the fall, asked Adam where he was and Adam was afraid because he was naked.

> "Shunning" = Hebrew word *sûr* = to turn aside, depart[7]
>
> "Evil" = Hebrew word *ra'* = bad, evil, malignant, unpleasant, distress, misery, injury, calamity, etc.[8] It is first mentioned in Genesis 2:9 in reference to the Tree of the Knowledge of Good and Evil.

When looked at collectively, these characteristics give a picture of a man who was morally above reproach, keeping his nose clean at every turn, keeping away from everything with the potential to contaminate him in any way and who was actually in fear of God. It could be a fear in the sense of reverence to God but, I believe, much like when Adam saw his condition after the fall, Job was actually afraid of God and His righteous judgements. He did not want to do anything wrong and wanted to be completely clean before God.

Job was also extremely wealthy as seen by his many children, animals and servants. He would have had to have enough land, homes and food to provide for all that he owned. This would have meant that Job would have been in a position of status and authority as well. Job was known as the "the greatest of all the people of the East" (Job 1:3 NKJV). "Greatest" here is the Hebrew word *gādôl,* which paints a picture of having great power, nobility and wealth.[9]

Amongst all of these descriptors, it does not say that Job was "sinless." He was blameless but the only human to be worthy to be called "sinless" is, of course, Jesus. Job did have knowledge of sin however. He also knew of God. In Job 42:5, it shows us that, in this earlier stage, Job had heard of God. It was not until later, however, that Job got to know God's love and character more intimately.

Job also had knowledge of burnt offerings. It was a very regular custom for Job to sacrifice burnt offerings for his children just in case they had "sinned and cursed God in their hearts" (Job 1:5 NKJV). In this, Job would consecrate and pronounce his children as being clean. Job 1:5 lets us know that Job did this continually. The Hebrew words *kōl* and *yôm* show this word "continually" was not any sort of exaggeration with *kōl* meaning "all, the whole, totality"[10] and *yôm* meaning "day, time, year."[11] No doubt, this was one of Job's full-time jobs. Perhaps Job was in a position acting as high priest on behalf of his family.

We will also find, as we read further into the Book of Job, that Job was a man trying to save himself through self-righteousness. He concluded that if he could just do everything right he could be saved. Job will eventually find out that he cannot save himself no matter how closely he follows the Law. Who knew that this book would have such a strong grace message! It is only by Grace that we are saved through faith in Jesus Christ and through His death, burial and resurrection.[12] Job will learn that he, too, is in need of a Savior!

Behind the Scenes

In Job 1:6, the sons of God come to present themselves before the LORD and Satan comes with them. Why would Satan be allowed to come before the LORD after having been kicked out of heaven? Isaiah 14:12 NKJV says, "How you are fallen from heaven, O Lucifer, son of the morning! How you are cut down to the ground, you who weakened the nations." Luke 10:18 NKJV has Jesus recounting how He saw, "Satan fall like lightening from heaven."

In Revelation 12:10 NKJV, it says, "Then I heard a loud voice saying in heaven, "Now salvation, and strength, and the kingdom of our God, and the power of His Christ have come, for the **accuser** of our brethren, who accused them before our God day and night, has been cast down."

It could be that this meeting between the sons of God, Satan and the LORD didn't happen in heaven at all. There are many accounts in the Bible where the LORD met with individuals on the earth. One example is when the LORD appeared to Abram in Genesis 12:7. The sons of God and Satan may have presented themselves before the LORD on the earth or in the second heaven.

Another possibility is that Satan was using a privilege once given to Adam. As a result of Adam's fall, Satan was legally able to operate in Adam's place of position. Thankfully, when Jesus was victorious through the cross, He restored the rightful position and authority back to us. We are now able to move in Hebrews 4:16 NKJV as those who can "come boldly to the throne of grace, that we may obtain mercy and find grace to help in time of need."

It is an interesting thought to ponder as to what would have happened had Adam not committed high treason in the Garden of Eden. Had Adam instead told the serpent to leave, would Satan have been forever banished from operating in the earth?

Other scriptures show Satan coming before the LORD. These, however, both happened before the cross.

> [1]Then he showed me Joshua the high priest standing before the Angel of the LORD, and Satan standing at his right hand to oppose him. [2]And the LORD said to Satan, "The LORD rebuke you, Satan! The LORD who has chosen Jerusalem rebuke you! *Is* this not a brand plucked from the fire? (Zech. 3:1, 2 NKJV)

> [31]And the Lord said, "Simon, Simon! Indeed, Satan has asked for you, that he may sift *you* as wheat. [32]But I have prayed for you, that your faith should not fail; and when you have returned to *Me,* strengthen your brethren." (Luke 22: 31, 32 NKJV)

Regardless of where Satan is permitted to stand when he is accusing the brethren, he is still the one pressing charges in the Courts of Heaven. Thankfully, however, we have a Great High Priest who intercedes for us when the accuser accuses us now.[13] It doesn't matter what accusations Satan hurls our way. If we come to God with it, He merely has to look over at Jesus and see that He has given us a spotless record and declares us not guilty!

In the beginning of the conversation that occurred between the LORD and Satan, the LORD asks Satan where he has come from. Satan replies that he came from "going to and fro on the earth, and from walking back and forth on it" (Job 1:7 NKJV). In similar fashion, First Peter 5:8 NKJV reveals that the "adversary the devil walks about like a roaring lion, seeking whom he may devour." Is this what Satan had been doing? While he was roaming throughout the earth, was he looking for someone to devour? Was he trying to find someone vulnerable?

Many people read Job 1:8 and perceive this as God saying, *"Hey! If you're looking to devour someone, why not devour Job? He could use to be knocked down a few pegs!"* This, however, does not line up with a loving God; One who gave Job a hedge of protection.

WHY DID GOD MENTION JOB IN THE FIRST PLACE?

Young's Literal Translation gives a clearer picture of Job 1:8. "And Jehovah saith to the Adversary, 'Hast thou set thy heart against My servant Job because there is none like him in the land, a man perfect and upright, fearing God and turning aside from evil?" Instead of thinking, that "Have you considered" was God pointing out a worthy target to the devil, would it not make more sense that it was actually more like, *"Is it because Job is so blameless and upright before Me that you have already been considering or setting your sites on him?"* "Hast thou set thy heart against My servant" as in the devil had already been thinking about how to devour Job.

In Job 1:9 and 10, Satan himself recognizes the goodness and care of God toward Job. He is aware that God placed a hedge of protection around Job, his household and everything he has. He also recognizes God's blessing upon the work of Job's hands resulting in his flocks and herds spreading throughout the land. The only accusation he brings against Job is implying that Job only fears God <u>because he is solely experiencing blessings from God</u>. Even Satan sees God's desire to bless and love.

The Request

Next, Satan makes his request. He asks the LORD [14] to reach forth His hand and touch everything Job has claiming that, then, Job would curse God to His face. Interestingly, the first mention of the word translated here, as "touch" is the same word Eve used in claiming she was not to touch the fruit from the tree in the middle of the Garden of Eden in Genesis 3:3.[15] It is not so surprising that the devil would ask God to touch in the same way he deceived Eve to touch the fruit. God, however, is not ignorant of Satan's schemes and, just because Satan asks or even dares God to do something, doesn't mean that God will do it. God does not take orders from Satan! Satan knew, though, that the LORD would have a legal right to "touch" all Job had because He was just in the judgement of fallen mankind. Satan, perhaps, underestimated the love of God and His plan for redemption!

What was the LORD's response to the devil's plea? It shows in Job 1:12 NKJV that He said, "Behold, all that he has is in your power; only do not lay a hand on his person." The word *hinnê*, translated here as "behold," is "used in pointing out persons, things, and places, as well as actions."[16] God was pointing out that Job had already made himself vulnerable. God did set a loving boundary, though, so Satan would not be able to hurt Job physically.

WHAT HAPPENED TO JOB'S HEDGE OF PROTECTION?

Tradition would have us believe that God removed the hedge of protection from Job so that, through the resulting hardships, Job would draw closer to God or learn something. Jesus says in Mark 7:13 NKJV, however, that tradition makes "the Word of God of no effect." We need to look beyond traditional teaching and see the truth of the Word of God.

The Word, in First John 4:8 and again in First John 4:16, clearly states that God is Love. First Corinthians 13 New International Version gives a description of Love. Some characteristics include, "Love is kind,"[17] "Love does not delight in evil,"[18] and "Love always protects."[19] We also know that "Jesus Christ is the same yesterday, today and forever" (Heb. 13:8 NKJV) and that God "does not change like shifting shadows" (James 1:17 NIV). God always has been Love and always will be Love.

This fact does not stop people from arguing that, even if God did not **approve** of all of the evil that came upon Job, He must have **allowed** it. They continue to state that nothing happens without God allowing it. Does this measure up to scripture? The Bible says in Second Peter 3:9 NKJV that God is "not willing that any should perish but that all should come to repentance." We all know that not everyone has come to repentance and that some have perished. Did God allow this? In a way, He did. Could He have stopped it? Not without violating His Word. He gave mankind free will; the freedom to choose between life and death. His desire, however, is for everyone to choose life. This was part of His statement in Deuteronomy 30:19, 20.

> [19]"I call heaven and earth as witnesses today against you, *that* I have set before you life and death, blessing and cursing; therefore choose life, that both you and your descendants may live; [20]that you may love the LORD your God, that you may obey His voice, and that you may cling to Him, for He *is* your life and the length of your days; and that you may dwell in the land which the LORD swore to your fathers, to Abraham, Isaac, and Jacob, to give them." (Deut. 30:19, 20 NKJV)

God is sovereign. He is above all. However, God cannot lie[20] and God will not violate His Word. He gave mankind free will. He will not revoke that nor go back on His Word concerning it. If God "allows" something, it is because to intervene and "disallow" it would mean going back on His Word. Many times, God "allows" something simply because we, in our free will, have allowed it. To illustrate this, one simply has to look, once again, at Adam and Eve. God had given them dominion and authority on the earth. They were supposed to protect the Garden. All Adam had to do was tell the serpent to leave the Garden and never return. Adam allowed that serpent to remain. God "allowed" it because Adam allowed it first.

If God didn't remove the hedge of protection from Job, then what happened to it? Nothing happened to it; Job got himself out from the hedge of protection. The hedge never changed. It remained the same and was always there at the ready for whenever Job would return. If only Job could have read Psalm 91 and Psalm 5:11!

Psalm 91 is known as the Psalm of Protection. The protection from God is readily available. There are conditions though. It is for the one "**who dwells** in the secret place of the Most High" (Psalm 91:1a NKJV). It is this person who is dwelling in His secret place who will then "**abide under** the shadow of the Almighty" (Psalm 91:1b NKJV). He, too, "**will say** of the LORD, '*He is* my refuge and my fortress; My God, **in Him I will trust**'" (Psalm 91:2 NKJV). THEN, that person will experience God's protection. **Because he loves God,** God will answer him, be with him in trouble, deliver him, honor him, satisfy him with long life and show him His salvation.[21]

In Psalm 5:11 NIV it says, "But let all **who take refuge in You** be glad; let them ever sing for joy. Spread your protection over them, that those **who love Your Name** may rejoice in You."

God cannot force His protection on people just as He cannot force people to receive Jesus. His protection and salvation are free gifts to any who will receive them. Job, however, did not yet have the Psalms to read and he had not yet learned the heart and character of God. As stated previously, Job, at this point in the story, had only heard of God.[22] He didn't know Him intimately yet.

How, then, did Job make himself vulnerable? How did he get out from God's hedge of protection? As we read throughout the Book of Job, one reoccurring theme is Job's self-effort and self-righteousness. Job seemed to believe that, if he was good enough and could follow the rules enough, he could save himself. Instead of putting his security in God and His shelter, Job put his security in all that he had and in his own ability to keep himself clean before God. Our security needs to be in God alone!

Job 3:25 NKJV gives us another answer: "For the thing I greatly feared has come upon me, And what I dreaded has happened to me." Fear was another reason for Job's vulnerability. What was Job afraid of exactly? Well, to figure this out, one needs to see what "came upon him." Job lost everything! Was he afraid that he would lose everything? Was he afraid that he would lose his ability to sustain himself and all of his belongings? Was he afraid that he would lose his livelihood? These are all possibilities. When we look at the continual sacrifices Job offered, however, could it be that Job was afraid of God's righteous judgements? That if he didn't keep everyone clean before God that God would bring judgement through His wrath? How many people today fear the same thing? Not knowing God's love and not knowing that Jesus satisfied the wrath of God on the cross, there are so many people who are afraid that God is going to set them up for a trial; a trial that would, perhaps, allow them to "learn something." This statement of Job, if it was a result of such a fear, was completely misdirected. Although Job lost everything, it was not a result of God's wrath. Job, at this point however, was ignorant of this fact.

Regardless of what exactly Job feared, the above is a far contrast from traditional teaching which claims God removed the hedge because Satan asked Him to. Never has God been in cahoots with the devil. Nor does God need the devil's help to teach His people.

WHAT DOES GOD USE TO TEACH HIS PEOPLE?

Does God use hardships to teach us? Can He teach us through hardships?

> [16]All Scripture *is* given by inspiration of God, and *is* profitable for doctrine, for

reproof, for correction, for instruction in righteousness, [17]that the man of God may be complete, thoroughly equipped for every good work. (2 Tim. 3:16, 17 NKJV)

[26]But the Helper, the Holy Spirit, whom the Father will send in My name, He will teach you all things, and bring to your remembrance all things that I said to you. (John 14:26 NKJV)

Along with these verses, multiple other verses instruct parents in teaching their children God's ways and how God has set people in positions in the Church to teach about God's Word and His ways.

This is how, according to scripture, God teaches us. However, when hardships come, God is able to use those times as teaching moments. He is able to turn what was meant for evil, into something good.[23] Similarly, when children experience a hardship, we can teach them too. It doesn't mean we wanted a hardship to come to them or allowed a hardship to come. For example, when my daughter was young, she received a new pair of rain boots. She was excited to wear them to school at the first opportunity. Knowing the sizing difference between the new boots and the boots she was used to wearing, I reminded her not to run in her new boots. Dropping her off at school, in her excitement, she took off running as soon as she saw her friends. She quickly tripped and fell. It was not my will that she fall; it was not my will that she got hurt. If it was, what kind of parent would that have made me; loving? I had even given my word in advance to try to prevent such an occurrence. When I helped her up, though, I had an opportunity to remind her why it is wise not to run in new boots.

In James 1, it speaks of various trials and how we should be joyful when they arise because of all the good that can come out of them. As we grow in faith, God will teach us in exercising our "authority muscles" and our "faith muscles." He guides us in exercising the dominion factor from Genesis 1:28. Believers have been blessed with the Word of God, the Name of Jesus,[24] the Blood of Jesus,[25] the Holy Spirit on the inside of them,[26] the gifts of the Spirit,[27] the fruit of the Spirit,[28] the Armor of God,[29] and the measure of faith.[30] He has also given us the authority through Jesus to use all of these tools. God will train us up in using all of the resources He has so graciously given to us. He gave them to us so that we could be victorious. And, where our ability to use these tools isn't quite enough, God's Grace is sufficient to get us across the finish line![31] This is why we are able to be in joy when difficult situations and circumstances arise! Jesus has already made the way for us to be victorious! It is one more opportunity for us to grow in our knowledge of using the tools in God's toolbox. It is one more opportunity for us to draw closer to God in the knowledge of Who He is and all that He has done for us. Nevertheless, we should never say or even infer that God has brought such trials our way.[32]

WHAT DOES SATAN ATTACK?

In the case of Job, it clearly states in Job 2:7 that Satan afflicted Job. What areas did Satan attack? The first attack was on Job's many oxen, donkeys and servants. As with each case, only one servant was left. This person was given the burdensome task of delivering the bad news. It is no surprise that Satan left someone available to give a negative report. Oxen and donkeys would have been used in working the land for crops. It would have been a means of business and income. It is a sign of self-sustenance. It is common to have attacks come on people's businesses and sources of income. It is a source of both identity and provision. In a business setting, a common attack could come in the form of slander or attacks on one's reputation. Because a "sword" in the Bible often refers to "words or tongue," the servants being killed by the sword in Job 1:15, could possibly, in present day, represent such a slanderous attack.

The second attack was on Job's sheep and servants. They were struck by lightning. Sheep are a source of food and clothing. These are basic needs. The servants were a source of help. Much like today, it would have been a sign of wealth to have servants. Having many servants would have also indicated a position of authority and status. In this instance, therefore, both basic needs and position were struck.

Going further, the sheep and servants could also refer to the Church. Jesus often referred to His followers as sheep and their leadership as shepherds. The sheep would have been, quite literally, used for the burnt offerings as well. People's spiritual needs and position are often readily attacked.

The third attack came upon the camels. These, like the oxen and donkeys, were stolen. The servants involved were also killed by the sword. Camels were used for transportation. They could have been a means of transporting goods. It would have meant another avenue of provision was affected.

The fourth attack came upon family. All of Job's ten children were killed. It is no surprise that with this final report Job responded in the way he did.

What was Satan's intention with these attacks?

Satan's intent was to drive Job away from God, to make Job believe that God is unjust and to make Job look at himself and his circumstances rather than looking to God. It is a well-used strategy of his to get people to look horizontally rather than vertically. His main objective, however, is always to steal, kill and destroy.

It is interesting to note that, through the attacks; Job's belongings were literally stolen, killed and destroyed. Satan's strategies have not changed. John 10:10 NKJV gives it to us straight, "The thief does not come except to steal, and to kill, and to destroy. I have come that they may have life, and that they may have *it* more abundantly." Even if Job 2:7 didn't confirm it, these attacks had Satan's "fingerprints" all over them. Second Corinthians 2:11 warns that we should be aware of the ploys Satan uses so as not to be duped by him.

WHAT WAS JOB'S RESPONSE?

Job 1:20 NKJV says, "Then Job arose, and rent his mantle, and shaved his head, and fell down upon the ground and worshipped." The word translated "mantle" could refer to a "garment worn over a tunic by men of rank" or even "the garment of the high priest."[33] The first reference to that Hebrew word in the Bible is in Exodus 28:4 in describing the high priest's garments. This, along with the numerous sacrifices Job did, is yet another hint to the possibility that Job could have been operating in the role as high priest for his family.

At least Job continued to worship! Or did he? The Hebrew word *šāḥâ* while it means "to bow oneself down," can also mean, "to sink down, to be depressed."[34] This same word was used in Proverbs 12:25 NKJV saying, "Anxiety in the heart of man causes depression, But a good word makes it glad." As stated above, Satan often tries to get people to look horizontally (comparing yourself to others, focusing on circumstances around you) rather than looking vertically (to God and His love). If you look at circumstances and bad reports, it leads to depression. Look vertically! Just like Peter in Matthew

14:29-33, when he focused on Jesus, he walked on the water. When he looked at the troubling wind and the waves, he started to sink.

Depression would explain the following verse better than worship. Job 1:21 NKJV states, "Naked I came from my mother's womb, And naked shall I return there. The LORD gave, and the LORD has taken away; Blessed be the name of the LORD." This is one of the most widely quoted scriptures from the Book of Job. It is true that it is in the Bible. It is true that Job said it. However, it is not an entirely true statement. The LORD did not take anything away from Job.[35] Job, however, in not knowing the behind the scenes, was speaking out of ignorance and depression. Job later admits to having spoken incorrectly in Job 42:3.

Furthermore, in Job 1:22 NKJV, it says, "In all this Job did not sin nor charge God with wrong." People have long thought that, if Job wasn't charged with sin, Job must have been right in what he said. If we look at the first time the word translated here as "sin" was used in the Bible it might shed some light on the phrase in question. It was first used in Genesis 20:6 NKJV where God reveals to Abimelech in a dream, "Yes, I know that you did this in the integrity of your heart. For I also withheld you from sinning against Me; therefore I did not let you touch her." Could it be it wasn't counted as sin because it came from an innocent ignorance?

---

1 Bullock, Robin D. *God is Absolutely Good* (Warrior, Alabama: YFMCI Publishing, 2010), 84.
2 "H347 - 'iyôḇ - Strong's Hebrew Lexicon (kjv)." Blue Letter Bible. Web. 26 Aug, 2021.
https://www.blueletterbible.org/lexicon/h347/kjv/wlc/0-1/ .
3 "H8535 - tām - Strong's Hebrew Lexicon (nkjv)." Blue Letter Bible. Web. 23 Aug, 2021.
https://www.blueletterbible.org/lexicon/h8535/nkjv/wlc/0-1/ .

4 "H8535 - tām – Gesenius' Hebrew-Chaldee Lexicon (nkjv)." Blue Letter Bible. Web. 27 Aug, 2021.
https://www.blueletterbible.org/lexicon/h8535/nkjv/wlc/0-1/ .
5 "H3477 - yāšār - Strong's Hebrew Lexicon (nkjv)." Blue Letter Bible. Web. 23 Aug, 2021.
https://www.blueletterbible.org/lexicon/h3477/nkjv/wlc/0-1/ .
6 "H3372 - yārē' - Strong's Hebrew Lexicon (nkjv)." Blue Letter Bible. Accessed 23 Aug, 2021.
https://www.blueletterbible.org/lexicon/h3372/nkjv/wlc/0-1/
7 "H5493 - sûr - Strong's Hebrew Lexicon (nkjv)." Blue Letter Bible. Accessed 23 Aug, 2021.
https://www.blueletterbible.org/lexicon/h5493/nkjv/wlc/0-1/
8 "H7451 - raʿ - Strong's Hebrew Lexicon (nkjv)." Blue Letter Bible. Accessed 23 Aug, 2021.
https://www.blueletterbible.org/lexicon/h7451/nkjv/wlc/0-1/
9 "H1419 - gāḏôl - Strong's Hebrew Lexicon (nkjv)." Blue Letter Bible. Accessed 26 Aug, 2021.
https://www.blueletterbible.org/lexicon/h1419/nkjv/wlc/0-1/
10 "H3605 - kōl - Strong's Hebrew Lexicon (nkjv)." Blue Letter Bible. Accessed 13 Mar, 2025.
https://www.blueletterbible.org/lexicon/h3605/nkjv/wlc/0-1/
11 "H3117 - yôm - Strong's Hebrew Lexicon (nkjv)." Blue Letter Bible. Accessed 26 Aug, 2021.
https://www.blueletterbible.org/lexicon/h3117/nkjv/wlc/0-1/
12 See Eph. 2:8
13 Heb. 7:25, Rom. 8:34
14 In his book, *God is Absolutely Good*, Robin D. Bullock explains the difference between the titles of Elohim and YHVH and how they are written in the KJV of the Bible. When the Bible prints LORD, it is translating YHVH. Prophet Bullock details how the LORD describes God and His governmental system of harvest. For more information on this, please reference the book *God is Absolutely Good* by Robin D. Bullock. For simplicity in *The Lens of Love*, however, the author will use the Name "God" interchangeably even if it is speaking of YHVH.
15 "H5060 - nāḡaʿ - Strong's Hebrew Lexicon (nkjv)." Blue Letter Bible. Accessed 26 Aug, 2021.
https://www.blueletterbible.org/lexicon/h5060/nkjv/wlc/0-1/
16 "H2009 - hinnê – Gesenius' Hebrew-Chaldee Lexicon (nkjv)." Blue Letter Bible. Accessed 26 Aug, 2021.
https://www.blueletterbible.org/lexicon/h2009/nkjv/wlc/0-1/
17 See 1 Cor. 13:4 NIV
18 See 1 Cor. 13:6 NIV
19 See 1 Cor. 13:7 NIV
20 See Num. 23:19, 1 Sam. 15:29
21 See Psalm 91:14-16 NKJV
22 See Job 42:5
23 See Gen. 50:20
24 See John 14:13, 14
25 See Rom. 5:9

26 See Rom. 8:11
27 See 1 Cor. 12:1-11
28 See Gal. 5:22, 23
29 See Eph. 6:13-18
30 See Rom. 12:3
31 See 2 Cor. 12:9 NKJV
32 See James 1:13
33 "H4598 - mᵊʿîl - Strong's Hebrew Lexicon (nkjv)." Blue Letter Bible. Accessed 26 Aug, 2021. https://www.blueletterbible.org/lexicon/h4598/nkjv/wlc/0-1/
34 "H7812 - šāḥâ – Gesenius' Hebrew-Chaldee Lexicon (nkjv)." Blue Letter Bible. Accessed 26 Aug, 2021. https://www.blueletterbible.org/lexicon/h7812/nkjv/wlc/0-1/
35 See Job 2:7. Another view could be to see that the reference to the LORD was referring to the system of government in which one reaps what has been sown. In this case, Satan was enabled to demand a harvest of seed sown by Job. Even in this case, it is not God's perfect will for Job to have destruction come to him and it is still Satan doing the stealing, killing and destroying. For more information on this system of government, please refer to *God is Absolutely Good* by Robin D. Bullock.

Chapter Two

JOB CHAPTER 2

ANOTHER PEEK BEHIND THE SCENES

Chapter two of the Book of Job shows yet another peek behind the scenes. The scene presents itself as almost a replay of the first scene. The sons of God present themselves before the LORD and Satan comes too. The LORD repeats His question asking Satan from where he has come. Once again, Satan admits that he came from "roaming throughout the earth, going back and forth on it" (Job 2:2 NIV). God's next question remains the same as previously discussed but with a new addition.

> And Jehovah saith unto the Adversary,
> 'Hast thou set thy heart unto My servant

> Job because there is none like him in the land, a man perfect and upright, fearing God and turning aside from evil? and still he is keeping hold on his integrity, and thou dost move Me against him to swallow him up for nought!' (Job 2:3 YLT)

We find here that God speaks of a quality in Job that has been revealed during this difficult time. The Hebrew word used to describe Job keeping hold on his integrity paints a picture of someone continually, repeatedly pressing in and firmly seizing hold of and adhering to both integrity and innocence.[1] The qualities were always within Job but it was shown to be genuine through this time of testing. In other words, his integrity was proven to be sincere. Similarly, God's faithfulness had been proven to David before he ever stepped foot in the Israelite's camp. When Saul insisted that David use the king's armor for his battle with Goliath in First Samuel 17, David declined because he knew that God's faithfulness in helping him defeat the enemy had already been proven during his previous battles with the bear and the lion.[2]

God continues to say that Job maintained his integrity and innocence despite the fact that Satan "enticed" Him to "swallow" Job up "for nought." The word "entice" comes from the Hebrew word *sût*, which means "to incite, allure, instigate, entice, lure."[3] The first mention of this word is found in Deuteronomy 13:6-11 speaking of God's instruction to not listen to even close family or friends if they were to try to entice them to follow other gods. The Hebrew word for "swallow" is *bālaʿ*, which can also be translated as "destroy" or "devour."[4] The Hebrew word *ḥinnām* finishes the sentence rendering the words "for nought" as also meaning "freely, for nothing, without cause, gratuitously, for no purpose, in vain and undeservedly."[5] It can go even further to describe something done rashly.[6]

Are we, then, to believe that even though Satan enticed God to do something that He would simply do it even though He warned His people to not only not listen to an enticer but also to show no pity on them, not spare them and put them to death?[7] Not only that, but to actually destroy and devour someone undeservedly and without cause? Satan did try to lure God to destroy Job but it does not mean that God did so. Remember it is Satan who comes to destroy.[8] Knowing God, why would Satan even try? The devil is attempting to get God to walk in His rightful use of judgement of fallen mankind. Because mankind fell, God had every right to enforce His judgement to satisfy His wrath. God, of course, had a much better plan in mind; a plan of grace that was put in place before the foundation of the world[9] of which, at this point, Satan was unknowing.[10]

THE ENEMY'S RESPONSE

It seems as though Satan has a temper tantrum as his response to hearing that Job's integrity withstood all that he recently experienced. In Job 2:4, he implies that mankind will give up everything else to keep his life. Then, once again, he dares God to "touch" Job's flesh and bone ensuring that, when done, Job would curse or even reject[11] God to His face. Not only did God not fall for the dare, even after Job's body was inflicted, Job still did not reject or curse God. Satan is the father of lies.[12]

In verse 6, God once again responds by pointing out the obvious; that Job was already vulnerable. He did place a boundary for Satan to preserve Job's life. Even though Job was outside the hedge, God still showed His grace.

If there was any doubt left as to whom afflicted Job, verse 7 makes it clear, "So Satan went out from the presence of the LORD, and struck Job with painful boils from the sole of his foot to the crown of his head" (Job 2:7 NKJV).

Job's Response 2.0

What was Job's response this time? Job 2:8 shows Job scraping himself with broken pottery as he sat among the ashes. From where did this broken pottery come? Was it among the ashes too? Leviticus 6:24-30 gives instructions for the sin offering. Verse 28 states that "the earthen vessel in which it is boiled shall be broken" (Lev. 6:28 NKJV). Was this piece of pottery left from a sin offering? We know today that Jesus was our sin offering. We know that His body, His earthen vessel, was definitely broken for us. It is an amazing bit of foreshadowing to see Job getting comfort from a representation of the Savior.

The Wife

A new person is introduced to us next. This is the first time Job's wife is shown. If there is a question as to why Satan hadn't caused her to be killed along with the children, the answer comes with her dialogue. In Job 2:9 NKJV she comes to Job and questions him, "Do you still hold fast to your integrity? Curse God and die!" Not exactly the words of a supportive and devoted wife! She seems exasperated that Job hasn't completely turned from his devotion to God. It appears her words proved too useful for Satan to do without.

Job was quick to dismiss her words determining that she was speaking like a foolish woman.[13] After all, Psalm 14:1 NKJV states, "the fool has said in his heart, 'There is no God.'"

Job then posed this question back to his wife in Job 2:10 NKJV, "Shall we indeed accept good from

Job Chapter 2

God, and shall we not accept adversity?" Would this imply that, as long as she was living the good life, that Job's wife was tolerant of Job's obedience to God?

It is also significant to point out that Job is not referring in this verse to the LORD (YHVH/Yahweh) as in prior instances but, instead, to Elohim.[14]

Once again, Job is counted as not sinning by inferring the problems came from God because his statement was made out of ignorance. What if Job had given God the benefit of the doubt? What if he had known the true love and character of God? He could have responded so differently.

Job's Friends

We now are introduced to three of Job's friends who will remain with Job throughout the remainder of the book. It says in Job 2:11 NKJV that when they "heard of all this adversity that had come upon him, each one came from his own place—Eliphaz the Temanite, Bildad the Shuhite, and Zophar the Naamathite. For they had made an appointment together to come and mourn with him, and to comfort him." The three heard about the adversity that had come upon Job. The word "adversity" is yet another confirmation that these circumstances did not come from nor were approved of by God. As mentioned previously, there is an extremely long list of words used to describe this Hebrew word. It is once again, the Hebrew word *ra'* and means "bad, evil, malignant, unpleasant (giving pain, unhappiness, misery), wicked, distress, misery, injury, calamity, adversity, wrong."[15] This word is translated as "evil" 442 times and either "wickedness" or "wicked" 84 times.[16] God does not have any *"ra"* to give. First John 1:5 NKJV confirms "in Him is no darkness at all." God is opposed to everything associated with all that "*ra'*" encompasses. Why then, would He condone its use? **He wouldn't**.

WHAT WAS JOB'S FRIENDS' REACTION?

When the friends heard of all of the "*ra'*" that had come to Job, their initial reaction was to show sympathy and comfort. The Hebrew words *nûd* and *nāham* for "sympathy and comfort" describe nodding one's head and sighing deeply in order to show pity.[17] Verse 12 tells us that, when they saw Job from a distance, they could hardly recognize him. They began to weep aloud, tore their robes, and sprinkled their heads with dust, sat on the ground with Job for seven days and seven nights not saying a word to him throughout the week. This was their reaction to seeing how great Job's suffering was. Their focus was on the seen, the natural, the problem, the suffering. Their focus was not on God. Sympathy and focusing on the problem can lead to feeling sorry for oneself, a pity party and self-focus.

GETTING TO KNOW JOB'S FRIENDS

Eliphaz the Temanite, Bildad the Shuhite and Zophar the Naamathite all came to Job once they heard of all of the "*ra'*" that had come to him. Each, we will discover, speak from a similar yet distinct point of view.

Eliphaz's name means "my God is (fine) gold" and he is listed as being Esau's son, the father of Teman.[18] The people of Teman, according to *Gesenius' Hebrew-Chaldee Lexicon*, take their origin from the grandson of Esau and were famed for their wisdom.[19] Eliphaz does a great deal of speaking from the point of view of **experience and self-effort**.[20] He also represents people who rely deeply on their good family history or "pedigree." People, who focus on experience and history, are most interested in looking back to the past rather than looking in hope at the future.

Both Bildad and Zophar's names are only referenced in the Book of Job. "Bildad" means "confusing (by mingling) love"[21] and "Shuhite" refers to "wealth."[22] His main viewpoint seems to be rooted in both **tradition and justice**.[23] He represents, as well, people who rely on their wealth.

Zophar's name can mean "sparrow"[24] but could also mean "impudent."[25] "Impudent" can be defined as "not showing respect; shamelessly rude."[26] "Naamathite" comes from the Hebrew word for "pleasantness."[27] Zophar is concerned mainly with **legalism**[28] and can represent people who rely on themselves.

In the following chapters we will see how, while full of the best intentions, these three friends do in their quest to comfort Job.

---

1 "H8538 - tummâ - Strong's Hebrew Lexicon (nkjv)." Blue Letter Bible. Accessed 26 Aug, 2021.
https://www.blueletterbible.org/lexicon/h8538/nkjv/wlc/0-1/
2 See 1 Sam. 17:37
3 "H5496 - sûṯ - Strong's Hebrew Lexicon (nkjv)." Blue Letter Bible. Accessed 26 Aug, 2021.
https://www.blueletterbible.org/lexicon/h5496/nkjv/wlc/0-1/
4 "H1104 - bālaʿ - Strong's Hebrew Lexicon (nkjv)." Blue Letter Bible. Accessed 26 Aug, 2021.
https://www.blueletterbible.org/lexicon/h1104/nkjv/wlc/0-1/
5 "H2600 - ḥinnām - Strong's Hebrew Lexicon (nkjv)." Blue Letter Bible. Accessed 26 Aug, 2021.
https://www.blueletterbible.org/lexicon/h2600/nkjv/wlc/0-1/
6 "H2600 - ḥinnām – Gesenius' Hebrew-Chaldee Lexicon (nkjv)." Blue Letter Bible. Accessed 26 Aug, 2021.
https://www.blueletterbible.org/lexicon/h2600/nkjv/wlc/0-1/
7 See Deut. 13:8, 9
8 See John 10:10
9 See 1 Peter 1:19, 20
10 See 1 Cor. 2:8
11 "H1288 - bāraḵ - Gesenius' Hebrew-Chaldee Lexicon (nkjv)." Blue Letter Bible. Accessed 26 Aug, 2021.
https://www.blueletterbible.org/lexicon/h1288/nkjv/wlc/0-1/
12 See John 8:44
13 See Job 2:10

14 "H430 - 'ĕlōhîm - Strong's Hebrew Lexicon (ylt)." Blue Letter Bible. Accessed 13 Mar, 2025.
https://www.blueletterbible.org/lexicon/h430/ylt/wlc/0-1/
15 "H7451 - raʿ - Strong's Hebrew Lexicon (nkjv)." Blue Letter Bible. Accessed 27 Aug, 2021.
https://www.blueletterbible.org/lexicon/h7451/nkjv/wlc/0-1/
16 "H7451 - raʿ - Strong's Hebrew Lexicon (kjv)." Blue Letter Bible. Accessed 27 Aug, 2021.
https://www.blueletterbible.org/lexicon/h7451/kjv/wlc/0-1/
17 "H5110 - nûḏ - Strong's Hebrew Lexicon (nkjv)." Blue Letter Bible. Accessed 27 Aug, 2021.
https://www.blueletterbible.org/lexicon/h5110/nkjv/wlc/0-1/
"H5162 - nāḥam - Strong's Hebrew Lexicon (nkjv)." Blue Letter Bible. Accessed 27 Aug, 2021.
https://www.blueletterbible.org/lexicon/h5162/nkjv/wlc/0-1/
18 "H464 - 'ĕlîp̄az - Strong's Hebrew Lexicon (nkjv)." Blue Letter Bible. Accessed 28 Aug, 2021.
https://www.blueletterbible.org/lexicon/h464/nkjv/wlc/0-1/
19 "H8487 - têmān – Gesenius' Hebrew-Chaldee Lexicon (nkjv)." Blue Letter Bible. Accessed 28 Aug, 2021.
https://www.blueletterbible.org/lexicon/h8487/nkjv/wlc/0-1/
20 See Job 4:3-11; Job 5:8, 11, 27
21 "H1085 - bildaḏ - Strong's Hebrew Lexicon (nkjv)." Blue Letter Bible. Accessed 28 Aug, 2021.
https://www.blueletterbible.org/lexicon/h1085/nkjv/wlc/0-1/
22 "H7747 - šûḥî - Strong's Hebrew Lexicon (nkjv)." Blue Letter Bible. Accessed 28 Aug, 2021.
https://www.blueletterbible.org/lexicon/h7747/nkjv/wlc/0-1/
23 See Job 8:3, 8-10, 20
24 "H6691 - ṣôp̄ar - Strong's Hebrew Lexicon (nkjv)." Blue Letter Bible. Accessed 28 Aug, 2021.
https://www.blueletterbible.org/lexicon/h6691/nkjv/wlc/0-1/
25 "H6691 - ṣôp̄ar – Gesenius' Hebrew-Chaldee Lexicon (nkjv)." Blue Letter Bible. Accessed 28 Aug, 2021.
https://www.blueletterbible.org/lexicon/h6691/nkjv/wlc/0-1/
26 "Impudent." *Webster's New World Dictionary*, edited by David B. Guralnik, Elementary Edition, The World Publishing Company, 1966, 354.
27 "H5284 - naʿămāṯî - Strong's Hebrew Lexicon (nkjv)." Blue Letter Bible. Accessed 28 Aug, 2021.
https://www.blueletterbible.org/lexicon/h5284/nkjv/wlc/0-1/
28 Job 11:2, 4-5, 14-19

Chapter Three

JOB CHAPTER 3

WHAT WAS JOB THINKING?

Job 3:1 says it all concerning the verses that follow. It states that, "After this Job opened his mouth and cursed the day of his *birth*" (Job 3:1 NKJV). How quickly he forgot all of the goodness he had experienced. It was clear his focus was on himself and his present suffering. He was so ready to erase all of the blessings he had prior and skip to wishing he had never experienced any kind of life whatsoever – good or bad. Again, when one's focus is on self, it is easy to fall for depression's pitfalls. One such pitfall is to believe that all one's problems will be solved in death. In verses 13-19, Job begins to reflect on the peace, rest and freedom he believes comes to people both great and small upon their death. In the midst of his torment, he figured the only escape and salvation from it would be found in death. He goes on in verses 20-23 to question why life is even given to those who would see misery and hardships; who would rather die than live. In Job 3:23 NIV, Job goes further to reveal that he knew God's ability to hedge someone in and to hide and protect the plan for their life; "Why is life given to a man whose way is hidden, whom God has hedged in?" Does Job identify himself with having been hedged in and protected by God?

It seems verse 24 sums up Job's current state of mind confirming he is speaking out of depression. "For sighing has become my daily food, my groans pour out like water" (Job 3:24 NIV). The Hebrew word *'ănāḥâ* is found eleven times in the King James Version;[1] each time it is used to show deep, emotional groaning and sorrow. Job admits these groans have become his daily food. The Hebrew word *šᵊ'āḡâ*, which is used here as "groans," actually means the "cry of a wretched person, wrung forth by grief."[2] It is those cries which Job pours out like water. It is not a stretch, therefore, to reason that everything Job is quoted as saying is a result of his current emotional state.

THE FEAR

Job 3:25 NKJV reveals another layer into Job's thinking - "For the thing I greatly feared has come upon me, And what I dreaded has happened to me." We would not have to look far to find a similar scenario in our modern day. Tragic news comes to someone and they quickly admit that it was something they had always worried about or feared happening. Whether it be an instance of a bad diagnosis, loss of employment or even loss of a loved one, fear can often be found rooted somewhere within the situation. It would be easy to determine that fear was at the root of Job's circumstances as well. With further thought, however, would it be accurate to conclude that Job was really afraid of his entire empire being stolen, killed and destroyed? Was he truly afraid that all of his children would be wiped away in a single day? Instead, would it, perhaps, be more accurate to conclude that Job was, in fact, afraid of something else? Could it be possible, looking at all of the sacrifices he performed again and again and how he desperately tried to keep himself and his family clean from any spot or blemish, that he was instead in fear of seeing the wrath of God on his life?

How many times Christians behave in much the same way, we will offer up prayers for forgiveness repeatedly throughout our days often in the hopes of keeping ourselves clean before God. We live in fear of coming before God with a spot or blemish on our record. We don't stop to think of how graciously Jesus bore all of our iniquities on the cross[3] and how, when we received Jesus as our Lord and Savior, our record of sin and iniquity was washed clean for God to remember no more.[4] Hebrews 10:18 NIV goes on to affirm, "And where these have been forgiven, sacrifice for sin is no longer necessary." We no longer need to do as Job did and continually plead for forgiveness in order to keep our record clean; Jesus has already washed us and made us clean. We still repent and talk openly with God when we mess up and fall short. We do this, however, out of relationship knowing He is a forgiving Father. When we came to Jesus, God was "faithful and just to forgive us *our* sins and to cleanse us from all unrighteousness."[5]

This is in no way to be interpreted as condoning a continuation of a sinful lifestyle. It would be wrong to continue in sin with thoughts of some sort of blanket forgiveness. It is merely an attempt to contrast Job's sacrifices with how many look at begging for forgiveness. There are those who seem to play a game of ping pong with their righteous standing with God. They ask for forgiveness and feel clean, then they, for example, eat too much dessert and condemn themselves for gluttony (unclean). One can, no doubt, substitute a multitude of other suitable examples. Lobbing themselves back and forth from clean to unclean depending on the circumstances in hopes that when the day comes when they stand before Almighty God, they're on the clean side of the net. What if they miss a sin or don't know that they sinned? This is what Job had been doing with the sacrifices.

Perhaps Job recognized that, due to the fall of mankind, God's wrath was not yet satisfied; that a Holy God required justice for sin. So, when Job saw that everything with which he had ever been blessed had been removed from him, it is not hard for Job to surmise that the LORD had taken it away through His judgement. This is what Job had feared all along; that God would judge him and find fault with him.

It is no wonder that Job subsequently admits, "I have no peace, no quietness; I have no rest, but only turmoil" (Job 3:26 NIV). It is interesting to note that the Hebrew word for "peace" here speaks more of safety and security found in one's prosperity.[6] Job no longer had the security of his prosperity on which to lean. Now, he finds that he only has turmoil, which can be defined as "commotion and perturbation."[7] The definition of *perturbation* includes, "disquiet, agitation of mind, great uneasiness and commotion of spirit."[8]

If only Job could have realized that God was not the culprit behind all of the tragedy. Would Job have chosen, instead, to look to God for help in his time of need? Would he have brushed off the dust and trusted God to restore all that had been lost? Would he have ministered to his friends and encouraged them?

---

1 "H585 - 'ănāḥâ - Strong's Hebrew Lexicon (nkjv)." Blue Letter Bible. Accessed 28 Aug, 2021.
https://www.blueletterbible.org/lexicon/h585/nkjv/wlc/0-1/
2 "H7581 - šᵊ'āḡâ – Gesenius' Hebrew-Chaldee Lexicon (nkjv)." Blue Letter Bible. Accessed 28 Aug, 2021.
https://www.blueletterbible.org/lexicon/h7581/nkjv/wlc/0-1/
3 See Ps. 103:3
4 See Heb. 8:12 and Heb. 10:17
5 1 John 1:9
6 "H7951 - šālâ - Gesenius' Hebrew-Chaldee Lexicon (niv)." Blue Letter Bible. Accessed 29 Aug, 2021.
https://www.blueletterbible.org/lexicon/h7951/niv/wlc/0-1/
7 "H7267 - rōḡez - Gesenius' Hebrew-Chaldee Lexicon (niv)." Blue Letter Bible. Accessed 30 Mar, 2025.
https://www.blueletterbible.org/lexicon/h7267/niv/wlc/0-1/
8 Webster, Noah. "Perturbation." Webster's Dictionary 1828, 29 Aug. 2021,
http://www.webstersdictionary1828.com/Dictionary/Perturbation. Accessed 29 Aug. 2021.

Chapter Four

JOB CHAPTER 4

ELIPHAZ SPEAKS – EXPERIENCE/SELF-EFFORT

Chapter 4 opens up with Job's friends breaking their silence. Eliphaz the Temanite is the first to speak up. He dwells mainly on all the good Job has done in the past. Surely, all of Job's good works would be able to maintain his righteous status.

> ³Surely you have instructed many, And you have strengthened weak hands. ⁴Your words have upheld him who was stumbling, And you have strengthened the feeble knees; (Job 4:3-4 NKJV)

In verse 6, Eliphaz suggests that the fear Job has of God along with his integrity should be where he places his confidence and hope. Eliphaz concludes in verse 7 that the innocent and upright have never perished or been destroyed. Looking back at his own experiences, he states in Job 4:8 NIV, "As I have observed, those who plow evil and those who sow trouble reap it."

It is clearly seen that Eliphaz's point of view stems from self-effort and experience. He is convinced that as long as you do good works and keep far from evil, you will be kept free from the threat of destruction. It is a do-it-yourself salvation. It is very similar to the line of thinking Job always held. *Don't be concerned Job, you've done plenty of good works in your life. Surely, your current state won't continue much longer.* Eliphaz also has the platform of experience. In his many years, Eliphaz has gotten to know and see firsthand what happens to those who do good and to those who do evil. How many people do we know today who think they have it all figured out because of what they have seen in the past? Someone tells of how they are believing by faith for healing, for example, and someone pipes up telling of how they knew many with the same condition who died. These are the instances where one needs to look to Jesus and the Word of God and not listen to the sound of "experience." The experiences one has with God and His lovingkindness are those that need to be remembered. This is why the patriarchs would build memorials when God did mighty acts on their behalf. They would from generations to come see the

> The experiences one has with God and His lovingkindness are those that need to be remembered.

memorials and remember God's faithfulness and compassion. This would build their faith in knowing God would certainly be there again for them whenever the need arose. It is the experience of man's own conclusions that is the danger. It is dangerous to rely on experience to lead the way in forming opinions about present circumstances.

Note that experience in itself is not a bad thing. Experience is one of the main qualities people look at when determining an applicant's qualification for a job. People learn much through the experiences of life. However, the issue arises when one listens to the voice of experience over the Voice of God. It is when people categorize God's promises as untrue based on what they have seen through the "lens of experience."

DREAM OR NIGHTMARE?

Verses 12-21 in Job 4 tells of a nightmare that came upon Eliphaz. Was this dream from God? I would have to say it was not. Many times in the Bible, when God spoke to people, He would begin with instructions to fear not. Second Timothy 1:7 NKJV confirms that God does not give us "a spirit of fear, but of power and of love and of a sound mind."

Going on the premise that this dream was not from God, we must conclude its source was evil with the intention to sow fear and hopelessness. The dream gives little hope for mankind. What hope is there for mankind when even angels are charged with error?[1] Mankind is merely clay and dust; corruptible, fragile and fleeting. "Why bother trying," is the foundation of this message. It is certainly not a message of hope; a message of a Way, a Truth and a Life[2] for all of mankind. It is true that there is no hope for mankind to save himself. Nevertheless, the part that the dream neglected to mention was the hope that is found in God and His plan of salvation for all mankind; a plan that was from the foundation of the world![3]

---

1. See Job 4:18 NKJV
2. See John 14:6
3. See Rev. 13:8

Chapter Five

JOB CHAPTER 5

Experience Speaks

Eliphaz continues to reminisce about what he has known from experience to happen to people ranging from the foolish to the hungry. Then, he suggests Job do what Eliphaz would do if ever in his shoes. "But if I were you, I would appeal to God; I would lay my cause before Him" (Job 5:8 NIV). This advice comes just before Eliphaz mentions a long list of traits Eliphaz attributes to God. Eliphaz has concluded certain things about how God operates because this is what has been found to be true from what he has witnessed or heard in his life. "We have examined this, and it is true. So hear it and apply it to yourself" (Job 5:27 NIV). Eliphaz begins the list of characteristics in Job 5:9 NKJV by proclaiming of God that He "does great things, and unsearchable, Marvelous things without number." He continues to speak of God's provision and protection; His help for the oppressed and His dealings with the wicked.[1] He speaks of the victory found when you are right before God.[2]

A Closer Look

Job 5:18 NKJV seems to paint God as almost two-faced: "For He bruises, but He binds up; He wounds, but His hands make whole." The only way to view this verse correctly would be to ensure one is looking, once again, through the lens of love. Does a loving father beat down his children and then pick them up and dust them off? Certainly not and our loving Heavenly Father does not either! Let us remember that Eliphaz, like Job, did not yet know the behind the scenes. As much as he had learned about God's goodness, he hadn't learned that there was an adversary to which the "beatings" should be attributed. Additionally, we must not forget Jesus in our quest for answers. It was Jesus who was bruised so we could be bound up (as in bandage a wound)[3] and it was Jesus who was wounded so we could be made whole. Isaiah 53:10 NKJV confirms "it pleased the LORD to bruise Him." It pleased the Him because He knew the wonderful results that would come of it. Let us always remember Isaiah 53:5 NKJV, "But He *was* wounded for our transgressions, *He was* bruised for our iniquities; The chastisement for our peace *was* upon Him, And by His stripes we are healed."

---

1 See Job 5:10-16
2 See Job 5:17
3 "H2280 - ḥāḇaš - Gesenius' Hebrew-Chaldee Lexicon (nkjv)." Blue Letter Bible. Accessed 17 Mar, 2025.
https://www.blueletterbible.org/lexicon/h2280/nkjv/wlc/0-1/

Chapter Six

JOB CHAPTER 6

AND THE AWARD GOES TO...

The award for most drama-filled response goes to Job in the 6th chapter. He is still speaking from a place of depression and woe as he continues to look at himself and his circumstances. The words he speaks are not necessarily entirely true. It is true he said them and they are recorded accurately for us to read but it does not mean Job is speaking truth. He even admits in verse 3 that his words have been rash. And, in verse 26, Job admits once again that what he is currently speaking are the words of a "desperate one." The Hebrew word for "desperate" is *yā'aš*[1] and describes Job as being "void of hope."[2] He continues to blame God for inflicting him. He also continues to look to himself for any help. Just count the number of "I" statements in verses 8-13 finishing off with Job 6:13 NIV, "Do I have any power to help myself now that success has been driven from me?"

THE RANSOM

After his question, Job reflects on how useless his friends have been to him. Then, in verses 22 and 23, Job poses yet another question.

> ²²Have I ever said, 'Give something on my behalf, pay a ransom for me from your wealth, ²³deliver me from the hand of the enemy, ransom me from the clutches of the ruthless'? (Job 6: 22, 23 NIV)

Again, Jesus is the answer. Just like the kinsman redeemer in the Book of Ruth, Jesus is our Redeemer who paid the ransom for us all.³ Jesus is the One who would pay the ransom for Job. Perhaps he should have asked God to deliver him and ransom him instead of trying to do it himself.

WHERE IS THE SPOT ON THE SPOTLESS RECORD?

Verse 24 has Job giving his permission to his friends to, if they are able, show Job the "error of his ways." You can almost sense the sarcasm. Could he have been asking in sincerity? Certainly, he could have. No doubt, Job would want to know if he had strayed from his straight-as-an-arrow path. In his plea for "truth," He seems unconvinced that anything his friends could say would be of any real value.

In verse 28, Job asks his friends to look him in the face and see if he is lying. Then, once they are looking Job squarely in the eyes, Job makes his announcement.

> [29]Yield now, let there be no injustice! Yes, concede, my righteousness still stands! [30]Is there injustice on my tongue? Cannot my taste discern the unsavory? (Job 6:29, 30 NKJV)
>
> [29]Stop assuming my guilt, for I have done no wrong. [30]Do you think I am lying? Don't I know the difference between right and wrong? (Job 6:29, 30 New Living Translation)

"My righteousness" – there it is. This statement shows that Job is attempting to be righteous through his own self-effort. I believe the plea is sincere in as much as if he had strayed in any way to allow God to justly inflict His wrath upon Job, he would want to know about it so he could fix the error. However, I believe Job knew in his heart that he had remained upright before God and that his record remained unblemished.

Hopelessness

There is a reason for his hopelessness. There was nothing Job knew of to alter his current circumstances. He was already doing all he knew to do to keep his ways clean before God and that wasn't enough in Job's eyes to keep free from judgement. This is a common thread throughout the coming chapters. His friends figure Job must be guilty of something to justify what has come upon him. Job continues to try to convince his companions that he truly hasn't done anything to tarnish his record. He has done nothing to warrant a guilty verdict and the resulting consequences. Job even goes as far as to call God out as being unjust in His judgement upon him. However, in all of this it remains unseen by Job that "what has come upon him" is not a result of fault or sin and, more importantly, is not the result of God's judgement or wrath. It is simply an attack from the enemy to which Job made himself vulnerable. How frustrating it must have been for Job!

THE BLAME GAME

How many times have people blamed God for bad things happening in their lives when it was actually an attack? How many times have people searched themselves for wrongdoing to find what they possibly could have done to "deserve" such tragic instances? Most often, the blame is misplaced. Satan is roaming about seeking whom he may devour; to whom he can rob, kill or destroy. It is up to us to remain steadfast in God's unwavering promises so we remain stable and fixed and not make ourselves vulnerable to such attacks. When attacks are attempted, it is crucial we identify the true source and respond accordingly. God has equipped us with His Word, His armor, His gifts, His angels and an endless arsenal to both defend ourselves against and resist such attacks. We must never forget that if we merely resist the devil he will flee from us.[4]

---

1 "H2976 - yā'aš - Strong's Hebrew Lexicon (nkjv)." Blue Letter Bible. Accessed 31 Aug, 2021.
https://www.blueletterbible.org/lexicon/h2976/nkjv/wlc/0-1/
2 "H2976 - yā'aš - Gesenius' Hebrew-Chaldee Lexicon (nkjv)." Blue Letter Bible. Accessed 31 Aug, 2021.
https://www.blueletterbible.org/lexicon/h2976/nkjv/wlc/0-1/
3 See Matt. 20:28, Mark 10:45, 1 Tim 2:6
4 See James 4:7

Chapter Seven

JOB CHAPTER 7

IS THERE ANY HOPE?

Chapter 7 is a continuation of Job's queries. It seems as though he has summed up his existence as one who lived a hard life. Has his present circumstances clouded any memory of the prosperity and peace he knew for the majority of his life? In Job7:3 NIV, his focus is on the "months of futility and nights of misery" that he believes were assigned to him. Focusing on all that is wrong in life can certainly give anyone such a viewpoint. It is so easy for us to think there is no hope when in the midst of all our senses screaming at us. Job goes on to describe his current physical state including insomnia, being covered in "worms and scabs" and having broken and festering skin.[1] Many of these would be difficult to ignore or look beyond. This is where hope is such a help; the ability to look beyond present circumstances to a better future. This is also the perfect time to look back and remember all of the times you were delivered out of bad situations. Knowing that God was faithful then helps immensely in being certain He will be faithful now and always. The choice is ours upon that which we dwell. It may be difficult but it is far greater to remain in hope. Job's choice in chapter 7 is clear. He sees his days coming "to an end without hope"[2] and that his "eyes will never see happiness again."[3] Because of this, he proclaims in Job 7:11 NKJV that he will not only not keep silent, but also will "speak in the anguish of [his] spirit" and "complain in the bitterness of [his] soul." These are more examples of "words without knowledge."

YOU'RE BEING WATCHED!

Job reveals to us something that he has noticed. He has concluded that God watches over Job unceasingly.[4] In error, still because Job is ignorant to all those operating behind the scenes, he accuses God of giving nightmares and fear-producing visions.[5] However, that aside, Job is aware that God watches over him. Job figures, though, that God is watching out of judgement more so than out of His tender love and mercy. Job 7:18 NIV confirms this when Job states that God "examines him every morning and test[s] him every moment." Some translations even show Job calling God the "Watcher of Men."[6]

WHAT HAVE I DONE?

Job has tried desperately throughout his entire life to live righteously and now he asks, "<u>If</u> I have sinned, what have I done?"[7] Again, Job is wondering what he did to warrant the judgement of God to come upon him. He doesn't know of anything. Job was living in self-effort and depending on his own self-righteousness. Then, he asks why God hasn't pardoned his offenses and forgiven his sins.[8] Job likely figured he had clearly done enough sacrifices to cover any offenses and sins. After all, he did sacrifices continually! Still, the circumstance he was enduring wasn't brought about through a punishment for sin. It was an attack from the enemy. Thankfully, today we know that, through Jesus, all our offenses and sins have been washed away and we can rely on Jesus' righteousness instead of our own.

---

1 See Job 7:4, 5
2 Job 7:6 NIV
3 Job 7:7 NIV
4 See Job 7:17-19 NIV
5 See Job 7:14
6 Job 7:18 NKJV
7 See Job 7:20 NIV
8 See Job 7:21

Chapter Eight

JOB CHAPTER 8

BILDAD – JUSTICE

It is in chapter 8 where we first hear from Bildad the Shuhite. Until now, it seems as though he has remained silent. Bildad sums up Job's discourse as words that resemble a "strong wind."[1] He even questions Job on how long he will continue speaking such things. It seems Bildad has heard enough and could keep his silence no longer.

As stated previously, one of the viewpoints from which Bildad speaks is justice. Justice says that there must be a penalty for sin. Without payment for sin, justice is not satisfied. Justice also says that if you don't sin, you are blessed and will not incur destructive consequences. Running throughout the

Book of Job can be found a court case of sorts. One can see the spiritual justice system at work.

Putting on his legal hat, Bildad brings us to the courtroom. He asks his opening questions in Job 8:3 NKJV, "Does God subvert judgment? Or does the Almighty pervert justice?" Then, Bildad signals to Job to look at his own children sitting in their roles as defendants. Accused of sin, a guilty verdict is handed down and a death penalty is carried out.[2] The next case is then brought before the Judge. Job now stands accused. Bildad assures him that he can plead with God and, if Job is in fact pure and upright, God will, righteously and with justice, restore Job to his rightful place.[3] The ensuing restoration would then, according to verse 7, bring such prosperity to Job that the plenty he experienced at the start of his life would seem small.

BILDAD – TRADITION

Bildad starts looking through the lens of tradition to find answers.

> [8]Ask the former generations and find out what their fathers learned, [9]for we were born only yesterday and know nothing, and our days on earth are but a shadow. [10]Will they not instruct you and tell you? Will they not bring forth words from their understanding? (Job 8:8-10 NIV)

Although we can certainly learn from the past and from older generations, we should always seek God first and foremost. It says in James 1:5 that if we lack wisdom, God will generously give it to any who will just ask Him. There are many scriptures instructing parents to teach their children the ways and purposes of God. The danger comes when people start depending on words that have been handed down and handed down which either have no foundation in God or have been so muddled through the "generational telephone game" it no longer represents God's truth.

Standing on such baseless tradition is much like what is seen in the verses that follow. The people who forget God and His ways are compared to hollow reeds and foundationless papyrus.[4] They may look good for a while but their hope is as strong as a spider's web; it cannot be relied upon to hold you up when you need support.[5]

JUSTICE IN ACTION

Next, Bildad likens a person to a well-cared for plant.[6] Like those who rely on God, this plant is in good soil, is well watered and given plenty of light. Whether they are deceived or blinded to the excellent care and conditions they have, some will start to seek a different source. The plant which Bildad describes started seeking nourishment from rocks and stones.[7] The result was only to have the plant "torn from its spot, that place [disown] it and [say], 'I never saw you.' Surely its life withers away, and from the soil other plants grow" (Job 8:18, 19 NIV).

What? Is Bildad implying that our loving God would completely cut off anyone who turns away from Him with no further hope? No, that is what justice does when the penalty is not satisfied. Thankfully, Jesus paid the penalty for our sin in full. Justice was satisfied when Jesus took all of the punishment for us. Now, we can return to God just as the prodigal son did in Luke 15:20-24. The Father is waiting in great anticipation for those moments. The only time we see people torn from their place without future hope is when people know the loving care of the Father, refuse it, and refuse to receive what Jesus did for them. Receiving the gift of righteousness that Jesus purchased for us is a choice.

God will not force it upon anyone. So, if someone chooses to do without Jesus and God's plan of redemption, justice still cries out. As it was with the plant, it thrived so long as it was receiving God's care. However, it chose to seek life apart from the Giver of Life and rejected the help that could only be found in Him. It was then that it was ripped out. Justice was served.

Bildad seems confident that there is great hope for Job if he is as upright and blameless as he claims.

> [20]Behold, God will not cast away the blameless, Nor will He uphold the evildoers. [21]He will yet fill your mouth with laughing, And your lips with rejoicing. [22]Those who hate you will be clothed with shame, And the dwelling place of the wicked will come to nothing. (Job 8:20-22 NKJV)

Justice has two sides. It can bring much sorrow and condemnation to the guilty. However, it can be a source of much victory and validation when one is vindicated. Could it be this was Bildad's attempt at a pep talk?

---

1 Job 8:2 NKJV
2 See Job 8:4
3 See Job 8:5, 6
4 Job 8:11-13
5 Job 8:14, 15
6 See Job 8:16
7 See Job 8:17

Chapter Nine

JOB CHAPTER 9

WHAT'S THE USE?

Job responds in full agreement with Bildad's judicial viewpoint. In reading chapter 9, however, one must keep in mind that Job still isn't aware of the behind the scenes. Job still thinks that God has brought all of the torment into his life. With this thinking, Job's sense of hopelessness is understandable. Job figures it is futile to approach Almighty God concerning his present condition if God was the one who inflicted him in the first place. To Job, why would he try to reason a not-guilty verdict out of One whom, in Job's mind, had already counted him as guilty?

Job asks, "But how can a man be righteous before God?" (Job 9:2 NKJV). Oh, how blessed we are in knowing the answer! It is not our own righteousness but Jesus' righteousness which allows us to stand before God as righteous. We can be "justified freely by His grace through the redemption that is in Christ Jesus" (Rom. 3:24 NKJV) and, "justified by faith apart from the deeds of the law" (Rom. 3:28 NKJV).

A Direct Line

Job expresses the true greatness of our Almighty God over the next few verses. From giving orders to the sun and creating constellations, moving mountains and performing miracles, Job speaks of God's infinite power, might and abilities.[1] He knows how pitiful mankind is in comparison to God's unmatched wisdom and profound strength. Job figures God is too high and lofty to be bothered with the plea of a mere mortal. This, along with many of Job's assumptions is, of course, untrue. God is love and He cares about His creation. How many times does God instruct in His Word for us to call upon Him and He promises to answer us? Psalms 17:6, 50:15, 91:15, 120:1 and Jeremiah 29:12 are just a few times. Growing up, I knew Jeremiah 33:3 NKJV as 'God's phone number', "Call to Me, and I will answer you, and show you great and mighty things, which you do not know." Why did Job think God wouldn't listen to him? It is because Job thought that it was God who had inflicted him. He thought God counted him among the guilty. In Job's mind, there were no appeals in this court of law. There was no room for changing a verdict.

A Reason for Hope

Job continues to stand on his self-righteousness and blamelessness. Job 9:20, 21 Revised Standard Version says, "Though I am innocent, my own mouth would condemn me; though I am blameless, he would prove me perverse." Is Job actually calling God unjust? It seems so.

There is only room left for hopelessness at this point. "I know that You will not hold me innocent. *If* I am condemned, Why then do I labor in vain?" (Job 9: 28b-29 NKJV). Job continues in Job 9:33-35 NIV wishing, "If only there were someone to arbitrate between us, someone to bring us together, someone to remove God's rod from me, so that his terror would frighten me no more. Then I would speak up without fear of Him, but as it now stands with me, I cannot." Don't worry Job; there is hope yet. There is an Arbitrator: Jesus is our High Priest, Mediator and Intercessor! First Timothy 2:5, Isaiah 59:15-17, Hebrews 4:14 and Romans 8:34 tell us so. As we now stand in Jesus, we can come boldly to the Throne of Grace and acquire mercy in our time of need![2]

---

1 See Job 9:3-19
2 See Heb. 4:16

Chapter Ten

JOB CHAPTER 10

Puzzled

You can really see in chapter 10, again, where Job believes both all of the good and all of the bad in life come from God. He doesn't realize there is another in the mix. It must have been so confusing for Job. No wonder he asks in verse 18 why God even saw to it Job was ever born. *"Why allow me to live if You are just going to make it a horrible life?"* he seems to wonder. Job recounts the tender love and care God showed in making him and is quite puzzled as to why He would then turn and oppress Job.[1]

Job Chapter 10

BACK IN COURT

Speaking once more from his bitterness, Job returns to the courtroom. He asks that God not condemn him but to reveal the charges against him.[2] In verse 7, however, Job once again enters his not-guilty plea. He also continues in his hopeless lament that, regardless of his blamelessness, no one can rescue him from God's judgment.

Again, it seems to lead to such confusion for Job. Believing all good and bad come from God, Job wonders how a God who took such care in molding and forming him could afflict him so. How many others have thought the same when believing their bad circumstances were God's doing?

As stated previously, it is my belief that Job was afraid that, if he didn't keep clean before God, he would experience God's wrath. The circumstances in which Job now finds himself are, in his estimation, the realization of that wrath. So, the God who took such care forming and watching over Job prior to this time, seems to have flipped a switch to vent His anger against Job due to a guilty verdict. This guilty verdict, according to Job, however, is unfounded.

Again, allow me to reiterate that Job was considered blameless and upright before God. God did not render a guilty verdict toward Job nor has He shown wrath toward him. All of the negative circumstances currently being endured by Job are a result of the enemy's attempt to rob, kill and destroy. Job made himself vulnerable to such an attack through fear and self-effort. You can see the "fear-based" thinking of Job in verses 13 and 14. Job claims to know dogmatically that God would be watching him every second of his life. "If I sinned, you would be watching me and would not let my offense go unpunished" (Job 10:14 NIV). You can see why Job was continually doing sacrifices!

Verses 16 and 17 show Job's perception of God; that He will stalk Job to display His anger against him and even increase His anger toward Job. What a sad state. How hopeless it must be to think Love has turned against you. Job ends chapter 10 pleading for God to turn away from him so he can have a little joy before an even more hopeless end.[3] Thankfully, God never leaves us or forsakes us![4] There will be hope for Job yet!

---

1 See Job 10:8-18
2 See Job 10:2
3 See Job 10:20-22
4 Deut. 31:6, 8; Josh. 1:5, Heb. 13:5

Chapter Eleven

JOB CHAPTER 11

ZOPHAR – LEGALISM

The third of Job's companions speaks up next in chapter 11. His name is Zophar the Naamathite. As stated earlier, in our study of the second chapter of Job, Zophar's names can mean both "pleasantness"[1] and "impudent."[2] It is easy to see this latter characteristic in Zophar as he addresses Job. He actually seems to respond quite harshly. How can something be characterized as rude and pleasant at the same time though? The answer can be found in the form of legalism. The Law of God is pleasant; in its fullness, it points to Jesus. This is because it shows our inability to keep the Law and our need for a Savior. Trying to keep the Law in its totality through our own self-effort, however, is where we find legalism. This is also where the impudence comes in. Legalism says, "Seek God more! You're not doing enough! Do more!" Grace, on the other hand, says, "It is 'not of works, lest anyone should boast'" (Eph. 2:9 NKJV).

Measuring Up

Zophar echoes the words of legalism by telling Job what Job must do to make himself clean and to seek God more. First, however, Zophar tells Job where he has failed and fallen short. This is like the Law which shows us clearly that "all have sinned and fall short of the glory of God" (Rom. 3:23 NKJV). Zophar reminds Job that he has been professing to God that his "beliefs are flawless" and that he is pure in God's sight.[3] Then, Zophar shows that he desires God to condemn Job.[4]

Zophar continues to declare the greatness of God; His limitlessness and might. This is all very accurate and true. Our God is above all! Just like the Law, however, Zophar neglects to show God's mercy and grace. The Law is wonderful and pleasant but it is impossible to meet its demands without Jesus. Jesus was the only One to follow the Law completely and the only One to fulfil the Law.

To-Do List

In Job 11:13 NKJV, Zophar shows Job what he must do to follow the Law and save himself - "If you would prepare your heart, And stretch out your hands toward Him." In other words, "Follow God more." Then, in verse 14, he instructs to put away sin and not let any evil live with him. These are works. They are what we should all try to do; follow God and not allow place for sin. However, Zophar misses it by not saying, *"You need a Savior; you aren't capable of doing this on your own."* Instead, he promises Job that if he does manage to succeed in his attempts to fully meet the Law's requirements, "Then surely you could lift up your face without spot; Yes, you could be steadfast, and not fear" (Job 11:15 NKJV). He continues to paint a hopeful picture of a beautiful and peaceful life. There is a "but" though in Job 11:20 NKJV – "But the eyes of the wicked will fail, And they shall not escape, And their hope—loss of life!" So, you'd better look out Job. If you aren't successful in meeting these requirements, you'll be counted among the evil and the consequences will be certain.

---

1 "H5284 - naʿămāṯî - Strong's Hebrew Lexicon (nkjv)." Blue Letter Bible. Accessed 28 Aug, 2021.
https://www.blueletterbible.org/lexicon/h5284/nkjv/wlc/0-1/
2 "H6691 - ṣôp̄ar – Gesenius' Hebrew-Chaldee Lexicon (nkjv)." Blue Letter Bible. Accessed 28 Aug, 2021.
https://www.blueletterbible.org/lexicon/h6691/nkjv/wlc/0-1/
3 Job 11:4 NIV
4 See Job 11:5

Chapter Twelve

JOB CHAPTERS 12 – 14

FOUNDATIONS

Chapter 12 begins a response by Job, which continues until the end of chapter 14. Job has just listened to what his three friends have had to say. He seems frustrated by the fact that they are telling him what he already knows.[1] No doubt, as friends, their beliefs regarding tradition, experience and legalism have been discussed countless times before. These are likely the sandy foundations on which their lives have been built.[2] It is true that they all know of God but have they made God any part of their foundation? Up until now, most of what they understand of God is His mighty power and absolute justice. They, at this point, haven't yet recognized His mercy and love. Invariably, they end up attempting to meet the requirements for justice through their tradition, experience, legalism and self-effort. When the storm came, that foundation began to shake.

WISDOM EXPLORED

> ¹²Wisdom *is* with aged men, And with length of days, understanding. ¹³With Him *are* wisdom and strength, He has counsel and understanding. (Job 12:12, 13 NKJV)

The statement in verse 12 is put to the test closer to the end of the Book of Job. At this stage, however, it seems as though Job believes that wisdom and understanding come alongside people who have lived many years. It definitely should be the case that whomever relies upon the counsel in verse 13 should also walk in wisdom. Does this exclude the young; those who haven't had as much experience? As it says in James 1:5 NIV, "If any of you lacks wisdom, you should ask God, who gives generously to all without finding fault, and it will be given to you." This is a promise for anyone whether they are old or young.

As Job proceeds, he shows more of his views of God.[3] He certainly recognizes God's omnipotence and His position of Judge over all. How has Job come to these conclusions? It is through his personal familiarity with **experience** and **tradition**. "Behold, my eye has seen all *this,* My ear has heard and understood it" (Job 13:1 NKJV). He sprinkles a touch of pride on the top as well when he says to his friends, "What you know, I also know; I *am* not inferior to you" (Job 13:2 NKJV). **Legalism** comes next as Job turns to seek his time in court. "But I desire to speak to the Almighty and to argue my case with God" (Job 13:3 NIV).

This may be Job's desire but it is deferred as Job looks horizontally and focuses more on his companions rather than looking vertically to the Most High God. In verse 9, Job questions his friends on what the outcome would be if God were to judge them. It is such a common trait of mankind to do just that. Instead of examining ourselves, we are often so preoccupied with judging others. In addition, we also tend to judge ourselves in comparison to others. We may acknowledge our own faults but then we measure them against the faults of others. Job's friends being guilty would not make Job any less guilty. Verse 11 shows, once again, Job's fearfulness of God. He asks the others whether they would be in terror and dread if they faced a judgement from God.

Standing on his blameless and upright record, Job is certain that he will find vindication and deliverance once he pleads his case before God.[4] In verses 20-22, Job then makes two requests of God. The first is for God to withdraw His hand far from him and to stop frightening Job with terrors. We have established by now that it is not God's hand bringing fear or terror to Job so there is no response in answer to this first request. The second request is one Job should have made well before the three friends and he ever began their lengthy discussion. Job asks in Job 13:22 NKJV, "Then call, and I will answer; Or let me speak, then You respond to me." This is exactly what Job needs…wisdom from above.[5] Unfortunately, instead of waiting on God for an answer, Job continues to speak and speak and speak some more. The remainder of chapter 13 as well as the entirety of chapter 14 reminds me of a person who talks incessantly without taking barely a second to breathe and leaves no opportunity for anyone to get a word in edgewise.

Job Chapters 12 - 14

Purity

Job continues to reflect on how fleeting life can be. His speech is full of hopelessness. Although some of the points Job makes are valid, others are made through ignorance. We have the benefit of seeing a fuller picture than what Job saw in his day. So when, in verse 4 of chapter 14 Job says that no one can bring what is pure from the impure, we can see how God accomplished just that through Jesus. It is through Jesus that impure sinners were made pure.

> [25b]just as Christ also loved the church and gave Himself for her, [26]that He might sanctify and cleanse her with the washing of water by the word, [27]that He might present her to Himself a glorious church, not having spot or wrinkle or any such thing, but that she should be holy and without blemish. (Eph. 5:25b-27 NKJV)

> For by one offering He has perfected forever those who are being sanctified. (Heb. 10:14 NKJV)

Also, in Job 14:14a NKJV, Job asks, "If a man dies, shall he live *again?*" To him, it seems, he believed that once a man dies, they would neither "rise" nor "awake" nor "rise from their sleep."[6] Today, we know the glorious truth of Jesus' death, burial, resurrection and ascension as well as our hope for eternal life through receiving Jesus as our Savior. Oh, how hopeless we would be if we did not know the redemption God so lovingly provided for us all!

The glimmer of hope we do see in Job shows in verse 17 where he yearns for a covering for his sin. The offerings made before Jesus' death did just that; they covered sin. When Jesus was made a sacrifice for us, however, sin was removed from us. As stated in

Isaiah 1:18b NKJV, "Though your sins are like scarlet, They shall be as white as snow; Though they are red like crimson, They shall be as wool."

---

1 See Job 12:2, 3
2 See Matt. 7:24-29
3 See Job 12:13-24
4 See Job 13:18
5 See James 1:5
6 See Job 14:10-12

Chapter Thirteen

JOB CHAPTER 15

ELIPHAZ – TAKE TWO

Eliphaz decides to try once more to enlighten his listeners with experience. Firstly, he takes a moment to chastise Job. Even Eliphaz recognizes the rashness of Job's words and in Job 15:6 NKJV confirms that Job's "own mouth condemns [him]" and his "own lips testify against [him]." Again, he points to Job venting his "rage against God and pouring out such words from [his] mouth."[1] I hope it is apparent to all readers by this point that this book contains a record of what Job and his companions said and that those things were not all words of truth.

From the standpoint of experience, Eliphaz asserts that the aged are on his side as well as people older than Job's father.[2] He also implores Job to allow him to tell Job of what he has witnessed and promises he "will declare, What wise men have told, Not hiding *anything received* from their fathers" (Job 15:17b, 18 NKJV). He continues to educate Job from this perspective.

One verse worthy of noting is verse 14. It is worth noting because it once again points to Jesus. "What *is* man, that he could be pure? And *he who is* born of a woman, that he could be righteous?" (Job 15:14 NKJV). Jesus is that One who was both born of a woman and entirely pure and righteous. It is through Him that we are declared the righteousness of God. Second Corinthians 5:21 NKJV says, "For He made Him who knew no sin *to be* sin for us, that we might become the righteousness of God in Him."

ELIPHAZ' EQUATION

Eliphaz's experience tells of seeing the complete fullness of suffering and torment endured by the wicked and those who openly oppose Almighty God. It is an existence of hopelessness and ultimate ruin. It is no wonder why Eliphaz would conclude that Job must be at fault in some way. To experience, **A+B=C** all the time, every time. In this case, **sin + wickedness = judgement**. However, Eliphaz doesn't yet realize that what he is really seeing is **attack + not abiding under God's protection = suffering**.

---

1 See Job 15:13 NIV
2 See Job 15:10

Chapter Fourteen

JOB CHAPTERS 16 AND 17

It looks as though the three companions are overstaying their welcome. Job is quite exasperated by their speeches. He keeps looking horizontally as he stands in judgement of them. He claims he could "comfort" them in like manner if the circumstances were reversed. He goes on to say he would surpass them because he would actually speak words to them that would bring encouragement and true comfort.[1] Is this what Job is looking for from his companions? Does he simply want a sympathetic pat on the head? *"Now, now Job. It will be alright."* Even that, no doubt, would leave Job wanting. Quickly, though, he switches his focus back to hopelessness knowing that regardless of his silence or his speech, it will bring no relief.²

From verses 7-14, Job once again attributes all of his woe to God. The blame is once again misdirected. It is so vitally important for us to know the true character of God; that God is Love. This way, we know that a loving God would not be to blame in such an instance. We also know there is safety and security in running to God when negative and seemingly hopeless circumstances arise.

> It is so vitally important for us to know the true character of God; that God is Love.

Jesus is seen once again in Job 16:19-21 NIV, "Even now my witness is in heaven; my advocate is on high. My intercessor is my friend as my eyes pour out tears to God; on behalf of a man he pleads with God as a man pleads for his friend." Oh, if Job only knew the full truth in that statement!

> ¹My little children, these things I write to you, so that you may not sin. And if anyone sins, we have an Advocate with the Father, Jesus Christ the righteous.
> (1 John 2:1 NKJV)

> ²⁴But He, because He continues forever, has an unchangeable priesthood. ²⁵Therefore He is also able to save to the uttermost those who come to God through Him, since He always lives to make intercession for them. (Heb. 7:24-25 NKJV)

> ³³Who shall bring a charge against God's elect? *It is* God who justifies. ³⁴Who *is* he who condemns? *It is* Christ who died, and furthermore is also risen, who is even at the right hand of God, who also makes intercession for us. (Rom. 8:33-34 NKJV)

First John 2:1, Hebrews 7:24, 25 and Romans 8:33, 34 confirm that Jesus is both that Advocate and Intercessor for us. All hopelessness should flee when we find out that Jesus is both our Advocate and Intercessor! Sadly, not knowing this keeps Job in the depths of despair.

Where is your focus?

In chapter 17, he admits his focus is certainly on the problem rather than on the solution. "Surely mockers surround me; my eyes must dwell on their hostility." (Job 17:2 NIV) It is often too easy to dwell upon that which is in our view. Job was saying that mockers surrounded him. This gives a picture of having mockers in every direction around him. Saying, "must dwell," he gives a notion of having no choice but to look at them. If he were to simply look up and look to God, what would he see then? His focus would have shifted from dwelling on the problem to dwelling on the Solution.

Oh, but in verse 3, Job does cry out to God. The New Living Translation says, "You must defend my innocence, O God, since no one else will stand up for me" (Job 17:3 NLT). There is a lesson to be learned from Job. He knew who he was and did not waiver from that. In the first chapter, God declared Job to be blameless and upright. Even though all three of his companions as well as his present circumstances appear to be in outright contradiction to that, Job remains consistent in knowing he is in fact blameless and upright. He recognizes that if everyone else comes against him, God knows this truth.

Closing out chapter 17, Job gives the go ahead for his friends to give it another attempt in bringing light into the darkness of his present situation.[3]

---

1 See Job 16:2-5
2 See Job 16:6
3 See Job 17:10

Chapter Fifteen

JOB CHAPTERS 18 AND 19

BILDAD – NO MERCY

In Job 17:10, Job asks that his friends try again; to give another attempt to persuade his way of thinking. Bildad happily grants Job's request. Bildad once more brings his opinion from the standpoint of tradition and justice. He only speaks of the negative consequences faced by the wicked. There is no wavering by Bildad. There is no mercy; only punishment for the guilty. Tradition says that this is what we've always been taught so it will always be so. It stands dogmatically in its immovability of position of thought. Nowhere does Bildad even give Job the benefit of the doubt. Similarly to Eliphaz, Bildad has looked at the answer first and assumed what the equation had been. They have seen the results of what happen to wicked people happening in Job's life and figure Job is reaping "the reward of the wicked."[1] Psalm 91:8 NKJV says, "Only with your eyes shall you look, And see the reward of the wicked."

SEE OR BE SEEN

Why would the person in Psalm 91 only **see** the reward of the wicked? They would only see it as a witness; not experience it themselves. This is because they met the criteria at the beginning of the psalm.

1. They dwell in the shelter of the Most High[2],
2. They rest in the shadow of the Almighty[3],
3. They declare the LORD as their refuge and fortress[4] and
4. They say God is the One in whom they put their trust[5].

One can see that if Job was experiencing the reward of the wicked that only two explanations could fit. Either Job was wicked or Job wasn't doing his part in keeping under the protection of God. We know that God already called Job blameless and upright[6] so we can conclude that the latter is the case.

THE BIG IF

In Job 18:3 NIV, Bildad asks Job, "Why are we regarded as cattle and considered stupid in your sight?" Bildad likely felt this was true of Job because of Job's exasperation in response to them. Job, too, saw the result but knew wickedness on his part was not the "equation" in question. He did not understand the other possibility of being outside the divine protection. Job's conclusion at this point is that God has found fault with him whether justly or unjustly. This can also be seen in Job's response in chapter 19.

> ⁴And if indeed I have erred, My error remains with me. ⁵If indeed you exalt *yourselves* against me, And plead my disgrace against me, ⁶Know then that God has wronged me, And has surrounded me with His net. ⁷If I cry out concerning wrong, I am not heard. If I cry aloud, *there is* no justice. (Job 19:4-6 NKJV)

Job begins verse four with "And if." **If** he has in fact done wrongly seems a passing thought as he switches his focus to aiming his frustrations toward God. Once again, Job speaks words without knowledge while he waves his fist heavenward.

RELATIONSHIPS ATTACKED

It is interesting to see a brief mention of Job's wife in verse 17. The last we had heard of her was in chapter two when she advised Job to "curse God and die" (Job 2:9 NKJV). Here, Job reveals that, "My breath is offensive to my wife, And I am repulsive to the children of my own body" (Job 19:17 NKJV). The Hebrew gives a picture of Job's very existence[7] causing his wife to turn away from Job. These relationships have also become a victim of the thief who came to steal. It would have been horrible for Job's wife to have died along with their children but you can see how much pain must have come to Job in having his wife alive and yet turn away from him in this time.

In addition to that relationship being stolen, verse 19 shows that the relationships he had with his closest friends has also been taken. "All my close friends abhor me, And those whom I love have turned against me" (Job 19:19 NKJV). This shows that the attack from the enemy has continued. It did not stop with the devastations of the beginning chapters.

HOPE

The very irony in Job 19:23-24 NIV leaves me in awe! "Oh, that my words were recorded, that they were written on a scroll, that they were inscribed with an iron tool on lead, or engraved in rock forever!" If Job only knew that his words and this testimony would be included as part of the Old Testament and be studied for multiplied generations to come! Little, too, did he realize he would be prophesying the coming Messiah!

A glimmer of hope begins to peak through when Job pauses to dwell upon the precious promises he has stored up in his heart. Verses 25-27 show Job looking to the coming Messiah. That's it Job! Keep looking to the Redeemer!

> ^{25}For I know *that* my Redeemer lives, And He shall stand at last on the earth;
> ^{26}And after my skin is destroyed, this *I know,* That in my flesh I shall see God,
> ^{27}Whom I shall see for myself, And my eyes shall behold, and not another. *How* my heart yearns within me!
> (Job 19:25-27 NKJV)

Switching back to his companions, Job hands out to them a warning to close out chapter 19. "How dare you go on persecuting me, saying, 'It's his own fault'? You should fear punishment yourselves, for your attitude deserves punishment. Then you will know that there is indeed a judgment" (Job 19:28, 29 NLT).

---

1 See Psalm 91:8 NKJV
2 See Psalm 91:1
3 See Psalm 91:1

4 See Psalm 91:2
5 See Psalm 91:2
6 See Job 1:8, 2:3
7 "H7307 - rûaḥ - Gesenius' Hebrew Chaldee Lexicon (nkjv)." Blue Letter Bible. Accessed 27 Sep, 2021.
https://www.blueletterbible.org/lexicon/h7307/nkjv/wlc/0-1/

Chapter Sixteen

JOB CHAPTERS 20 AND 21

ZOPHAR – RUFFLED FEATHERS

Zophar cannot hold his tongue any longer. "Therefore my anxious thoughts make me answer, Because of the turmoil within me. I have heard the rebuke that reproaches me, And the spirit of my understanding causes me to answer" (Job 20:2, 3 NKJV). As we established previously, Zophar speaks from legalism and the Law. Up to this point, Job has been finding fault with the judicial system. Job tells of wicked people prospering and bearing no real consequence. Along with that, he sees his blameless and upright self bearing punishment after punishment. Zophar says in Job 20:3a NIV, "I hear a rebuke that dishonors me." The law has taken Job's accusations almost personally and is determined to set the record straight. Zophar is quoted in Job 20:4, 5 NKJV saying, "Do you *not* know this of old, Since man was placed on earth, That the triumphing of the wicked is short, And the joy of the hypocrite is *but* for a moment?" In other words, Zophar is saying that, in fact, the wicked get what's coming to them. Zophar determines to show Job that, regardless of what he believes, the wicked do reap what they have sown[1]. Throughout the remainder of chapter 20, Zophar describes, "the portion from God for a wicked man, The heritage appointed to him by God" (Job 20:29 NKJV). The dark commentary is in stark contrast from what Job has stated.

JOB UNCONVINCED

In chapter 21, Job seems steadfastly unconvinced by Zophar's speech. Job persists in bringing forth an opposing account of how the wicked remain in their wickedness as they seemingly thrive. Job shows the mentality of the wicked who seem to be enjoying life to the fullest. They put their trust in their riches and they refuse God. Life is so good that they do not see the need for God, or for a Savior.

> [14]Yet they say to God, 'Depart from us, For we do not desire the knowledge of Your ways. [15]Who *is* the Almighty, that we should serve Him? And what profit do we have if we pray to Him?' (Job 21:14, 15 NKJV)

You can see the deception to which these people have fallen victim. They have been set up to believe that, because they are momentarily successful, they can save themselves. They are so filled with pride they cannot see their need for God. In the end, they end up with the ultimate punishment – eternal separation from God. "For what will it profit a man if he gains the whole world, and loses his own soul?" (Mark 8:36 NKJV).

It seems as though Job has come back with his boxing gloves on. He is ready to fight and debate all that Zophar has asserted. Job insists that the wicked ways some people live by are largely disregarded; they live the good life without consequence.[2] He questions Zophar as to how often the wicked are actually punished.[3] Job concludes, however, that both the people who have lived a prosperous life and those who have lived in want end up in the same condition once they die. "Side by side they lie in the dust and worms cover them both" (Job 21:26 NIV). [This gives no room for thought of what happens after one dies. Their physical bodies may encounter similar treatment but not so for their spirits. It is a wonder what Job was thinking in this moment about Heaven, Hell and what truly happens after death.]

Job continues his debate with an extra dose of mistrust. He accuses Zophar in Job 21:27 NKJV saying, "Look, I know your thoughts, And the schemes *with which* you would wrong me." Job is not ignorant of Zophar's stance. The Law says that if Job has had punishment inflicted upon him, Job must be deserving of it. It is back to the equations of the previous chapters: Wickedness = Punishment. Therefore, if Job is experiencing punishment, Job must have been wicked. Job has been called both blameless and upright by Almighty God. Job has continuously given sacrifices in hopes to cover any and all sin. Zophar, speaking from the standpoint of the Law is adamant about calling Job guilty. Job is unconvinced and in closing out this chapter, Job simply states, "How then can you comfort me with empty words, Since falsehood remains in your answers?" (Job 21:34 NKJV). Is the Law capable of comforting anyone? Romans 3:20 NIV confirms that, "no one will be declared righteous in God's sight by the works of the law; rather, through the law we become conscious of our sin." Where in this could any comfort be found? Nowhere; it is only by continuing on through Romans 3 which teaches about being made right with God through faith in Jesus. "Therefore we conclude that a man is justified by faith apart from the deeds of the law" (Rom. 3:28 NKJV).

---

1 See Gal. 6:7
2 See Job 21:7-13
3 See Job 21:17

Chapter Seventeen

JOB CHAPTER 22

THE GOLDEN CHECKLIST

Eliphaz has his next statement ready. You can almost sense the tensions rising as the three companions address Job again. This time, Eliphaz comes armed with a long list of areas in which Job has fallen short. I call a list such as this the "Golden Checklist." This is a list of the things with which our own righteousness is measured. Many people have such a list without being fully aware of its existence. Christians are especially guilty of using the Golden Checklist as their chosen unit of measure. Have you gone to church this week? Yes? Then you get a golden checkmark. Have you prayed today; read the Bible today? Check, check. Are you in a Bible study?

Check. There are even, it seems, bonus checks for fasting and helping out with tasks that the majority consider undesirable. People then take their checks and add them up. How many checks they have determines their feeling of righteous status. Going a step further, these checklists can be compared to those of others to bolster an even greater sense of right standing. Such a checklist can also have the opposite effect. If there are areas in which checks are absent or if one finds they have insufficient checks to compete with others, guilt and shame and feelings of unworthiness can enter in.

While all of the dos on the Golden Checklist are good and often things we are called to do, we need to remember that the "works" of that list is not the way to true righteousness. Rather it is solely through Jesus exchanging our sin for His righteousness that we have become the righteousness of God through Christ Jesus.[1] We cannot earn our right standing with God. It is a gift of grace from Him.[2]

The Golden Checklist is similar to the list Eliphaz seems to have but not quite the same; it is the converse. Instead of measuring righteousness, he is measuring unrighteousness.

Eliphaz states that the charges he is about to bring up are not his own but God's. "Is it for your piety that He rebukes you and brings charges against you?" (Job 22:4 NIV). The indictment in Job 22:6-9 is as follows:

- taken pledges from his brothers for no reason[3]
- stripped the naked of their clothing[4]
- gave no water to the weary[5]
- withheld food from the hungry[6]
- sent widows away empty handed[7]
- broke the strength of the fatherless[8]

These charges and Job's implied guilt, according to Eliphaz, "is why snares are all around [Job], why sudden peril terrifies [him], why it is so dark [Job] cannot see, and why a flood of water covers [him]" (Job 22:10-11 NIV).

Once more Eliphaz shows his experience as he speaks of seeing the wicked punished and the righteous rejoice.[9] Then, Eliphaz implores Job to humble himself and submit to God. In other words, start adding golden checkmarks to your Golden Checklist! Job 22:21-25, 29-30 NIV give a peek at this list:

- ✓ submit to God
    - o prosperity will come to you
- ✓ be at peace with Him
- ✓ accept instruction from His mouth
- ✓ lay up words in your heart
- ✓ return to the Almighty
    - o you will be restored
- ✓ remove wickedness far from your tent
- ✓ assign your nuggets to the dust, your gold of Ophir to the rocks in the ravines
    - o the Almighty will be your gold, the choicest silver for you.
- ✓ when men are brought low you say, "lift them up"
    - o He will save the downcast
    - o He will deliver even one who is not innocent, who will be delivered through the cleanness of your hands.

It begs the question as to why Eliphaz did not have such an effect on Job. Did Eliphaz try to say,

"Lift him up" to Job or was he more concerned with tearing him down?

---

1 See 2 Cor. 5:21
2 See Eph. 2:8
3 See Job 22:6 NIV
4 See Job 22:6 NIV
5 See Job 22:7 NIV
6 See Job 22:7 NIV
7 See Job 22:9 NIV
8 See Job 22:9 NIV
9 See Job 22:12-20

Chapter Eighteen

JOB CHAPTER 23

UNWAVERING

What is Job's response to all of the accusations that have now come through Eliphaz? Did Job agree with them? Did he repent? Did Job stand up and argue with Eliphaz? Job did none of those things. Instead, Job expresses his yearning for an opportunity to come before God Himself and state his case. Why would this be Job's response? It is seemingly because, through it all – the circumstances and the accusations, Job remained constant in knowing who he is. Job did not waiver in knowing that he was blameless and upright. We could stand to learn a huge lesson from this. If we could, regardless of circumstances and accusations, continue to be aware of our righteousness through Jesus, we would not be so accepting of defeat and condemnation. Romans 8:1a NKJV says, "*There is* therefore now no condemnation to those who are in Christ Jesus." We would do well to remind ourselves of that when arrows of accusation are heading our way.

KNOWING IN PART

Job states in Job 23:4-7 that if he were able to present his case before God as an upright man, God would not press charges against him and he would be forever delivered. The issue Job faces, though, is in knowing where to find Him. "But He knows the way that I take; *When* He has tested me, I shall come forth as gold" (Job 23:10 NKJV).

Referring to his own "Golden Checklist," Job recounts the good he has done throughout his blameless days. Job knows who he is, but, does he really know who God is? Does he really know God's character and God's nature? It seems as though Job knows in part but not yet fully for Job is questioning God's just-ness. He still believes all of his troubles came from God. A judge who freely punishes the innocent would not be a just judge. No wonder Job speaks of his terror toward God. "Therefore I am terrified at His presence; When I consider *this,* I am afraid of Him. For God made my heart weak, And the Almighty terrifies me" (Job 23:15, 16 NKJV).

Chapter Nineteen

JOB CHAPTER 24

HEARING JOB'S HEART

The "unjust judge" seems to be a theme continued in chapter 24. Job tells again of how the wicked continue unscathed in their wickedness while the poor and needy suffer. "The dying groan in the city, And the souls of the wounded cry out; Yet God does not charge *them* with wrong" (Job 24:12 NKJV). Yet Job does reflect upon how, in the end, death awaits the wicked; those who oppose the light and love darkness. "He may let them rest in a feeling of security, but His eyes are on their ways. For a little while they are exalted, and then they are gone" (Job 24:23, 24a NIV).

Job's heart can really be heard, though, if one cares to listen to his speech. The way he seems to feel the pain of the poor and hurting. Job does not appear to take any pleasure in the circumstances they endure. There seems to be an empathetic tone to what he says. Perhaps where there once would have been mere sympathy, Job can now relate somewhat to the affliction of the poor and hurting of society. I would imagine that if Job was guilty of what he has been accused, he would find some satisfaction in seeing the hurting hurt. It is a backwards way of judging Job but it is also effective in finding truth. Looking at Job through the lens of love, one can see his love for mankind and his desire for the oppressed to be oppressed no longer. Why then, would anyone think he would willingly withhold or prevent help in someone's time of need? Eliphaz could have recognized his accusations as unfounded had he looked at Job through the lens of love. Instead, he looked at experience. Experience can be dangerous in that it can lump everyone into the same pile. *"In my experience, everyone who sees these consequences is guilty."* It leaves little to no room for grace or for exceptions. Job, however, will address the accusations further in coming chapters.

Chapter Twenty

JOB CHAPTER 25

THE VOICE OF JUDGEMENT

In between two lengthy discourses given by Job, there is a very short, to-the-point, response given by Bildad. Remember, Bildad speaks from the standpoint of tradition and justice. He undoubtedly feels that his point must be brought back into the spotlight. He chooses to remind Job of Whom he is directing his plea. "Dominion and awe belong to God; He establishes order in the heights of the heaven. Can His forces be numbered? Upon whom does His light not rise?" (Job 25:2, 3 NIV). Bildad is reminding Job that the Almighty Judge Who presides over the entire judicial system of the universe is so far above the ranking of Job. Bildad continues to cut

Job Chapter 25

deeper with ensuring Job knows how the human race is hopeless in its pursuit of right standing before such a Judge.

> ⁴"How then can man be righteous before God? Or how can he be pure *who is* born of a woman? ⁵If even the moon does not shine, And the stars are not pure in His sight, ⁶How much less man, *who is* a maggot, And a son of man, *who is* a worm?" (Job 25: 4-6 NKJV)

How right is Bildad in his opinion though? Should we just take him at his word? Let's start by answering his first two questions: "How then can man be righteous before God?"[1] We have the privilege of being able to find the answer in Romans 5:19 NKJV, "For as by one man's disobedience many were made sinners, so also by one Man's obedience many will be made righteous." The answer is Jesus! Likewise, "Jesus" is also the answer to Bildad's second question. As mentioned, when Eliphaz asked a similar question in chapter 15, Jesus is pure and was born of a woman. Bildad apparently had no comprehension of what God's plan of redemption was. Justice merely wants to be satisfied with a punishment paid. Bildad did not realize that God would become flesh through being born of a woman in order to qualify as a man to take the punishment for all mankind. As First John 3:2, 3 confirms, it is through Jesus that we can be made righteous and pure.

> ²Beloved, now we are children of God; and it has not yet been revealed what we shall be, but we know that when He is revealed, we shall be like Him, for we shall see Him as He is. ³And everyone who has this hope in Him purifies

himself, just as He is pure. (1 John 3:2, 3 NKJV)

When looking at Job 25:5, 6, I wonder where Bildad has come up with this viewpoint. Has God ever stated that the stars were not pure in His sight? When God made the sun, moon and stars in the Genesis account He saw it and it was good.[2] God even saw fit to use these lights as signs to mark sacred times on His calendar.[3] Wouldn't it, then, be fitting to question Bildad's statement in verse 6 as well? Does God consider man to be a maggot and a son of man a worm? If one looks at Psalm 8, it is easy to see God's true thoughts of man. The angels could even see it.

> [3]When I consider Your heavens, the work of Your fingers, The moon and the stars, which You have ordained, [4]What is man that You are mindful of him, And the son of man that You visit him? [5]For You have made him a little lower than the angels, And You have crowned him with glory and honor. [6]You have made him to have dominion over the works of Your hands; You have put all things under his feet. (Psalm 8:3-6 NKJV)

This certainly doesn't paint the picture of a maggot or a worm. So what happened? Instead of looking through the lens of love, Bildad is looking through the lens of judgement. All judgement sees, at this point, is mankind in its fallen state. It does not take into account God's love for mankind and His provision for restoring back to mankind the glory that they were created to wear.

---

1 Job 25:4a NKJV
2 See Gen. 1:16, 18
3 See Gen. 1:14

Chapter Twenty-One

JOB CHAPTER 26

SARCASM ANYONE?

Chapters 26 to 31 contain another lengthy speech from Job. It begins, as in chapter 6, with great sarcasm aimed at the three companions. This is seen especially in the New International Version.

> ²How you have helped the powerless! How you have saved the arm that is feeble! ³What advice you have offered to one without wisdom! And what great insight you have displayed! ⁴Who has helped you utter these words? And whose spirit spoke from your mouth? (Job 26:2-4 NIV)

He mockingly compliments the three for their lofty contributions to society and the "wise counsel" they have so freely given him.

GOD'S GREATNESS

Job's attention swiftly turns, once again, to address how he sees God Almighty. As we have seen in past chapters, Job focuses much on God's omnipotence and His omnipresence. Bildad, Eliphaz and Zophar are quick to remind Job that he is like a worm in comparison to God. Likewise, Job gives everyone a reminder of how much greater God is than anything or anyone else. There is no comparison to Him. Psalm 40:5 sums up what Job seems to be saying in the remainder of chapter 26.

> Many, LORD my God, are the wonders you have done, the things you planned for us. None can compare with you; were I to speak and tell of your deeds, they would be too many to declare. (Ps. 40:5 NIV)

From nothing being hidden from God in Job 26:5-6 to the wonders of creation in verses 7-11 to God's work in setting the constellations in place in verses 12 and 13, Job reminds all that these are "but the outer fringe of His works" (Job 26:14a NIV). Job characterizes these as some of the "faint whispers" we hear from God and questions, "Who then can understand the thunder of His power?" (Job 26:14b NIV). It is this power Job continues to describe in chapter 27.

Chapter Twenty-Two

JOB CHAPTER 27

FORSAKEN?

In past chapters, we have seen a court case unfold. We have also seen a plea from the accused to have his "day in court" to plead his case before the Almighty Judge. It looks as though Job has now concluded that he has been forsaken. Job implies that God has dealt unjustly by denying Job justice and by making Job's "soul bitter." [1] Could that be true? Through the lens of love, we have established that God did not inflict Job. Through the same lens, we can likewise see clearly that a loving and just God would never deny Job justice. We can see multiple times throughout God's Word including twice in Deuteronomy 31 that "He will not leave you nor forsake you" (Deut. 31:6, 8 NKJV). God's desire is to be in covenant with His people and to always be a help to them.

C*HOICES*

"But what about Deut. 31:17?" one might ask. Doesn't God say he will, in fact, forsake the Israelites He addressed in verses 6 and 8?

> ⁱ⁶And the LORD said to Moses: "Behold, you will rest with your fathers; and this people will rise and play the harlot with the gods of the foreigners of the land, where they go *to be* among them, and they will forsake Me and break My covenant which I have made with them.¹⁷Then My anger shall be aroused against them in that day, and I will forsake them, and I will hide My face from them, and they shall be devoured. And many evils and troubles shall befall them, so that they will say in that day, 'Have not these evils come upon us because our God *is* not among us?' ¹⁸And I will surely hide My face in that day because of all the evil which they have done, in that they have turned to other gods." (Deut. 31:16-18 NKJV)

If God desires a covenant relationship with His people, why would He have such a response? There must be more to this. God does not turn off His love for His people. It seems this instance is similar to what we discovered at the beginning of the Book of Job. God is always ready to have a loving covenant relationship with His people. However, if those people reject God, break their covenant with Him and decide to go it alone by living life either being their own god or by following another god, they put God in an unspeakably horrible position. Although God's love is unchanging and unconditional, He cannot force His protection on anyone. If someone turns from God and says they want to live life without Him, they also reject all of His benefits. They, as a result, leave themselves open and vulnerable to destruction and calamities. Once again, it is the case of people getting out of God's hedge of protection through their own free choice. As said previously, whenever those people turn back to God, He will welcome them back just as the father welcomed back his prodigal son in Luke 15.

KNOWING THAT YOU KNOW THAT YOU KNOW

Job continues his speech with defending himself and his integrity. It is encouraging to see how Job knows that he knows that he knows without any doubt, who he is and the quality of his character. He has just had chapter upon chapter of accusations flung at him and those indictments have not caused Job's opinion to waiver in the slightest. Likewise, we should be confident of our righteous standing through Jesus regardless of the allegations that say otherwise that come our way. That breastplate of righteousness in which we are called to clothe ourselves[2] is designed to protect our heart. "I will maintain my righteousness and never let go of it; my conscience will not reproach me as long as I live" (Job 27:6 NIV). The issue Job has is that he is depending on his own righteousness. Thankfully, today, we can rely on the much greater gift of Jesus' righteousness.

Job then proceeds to educate his listeners. "I will teach you about the hand of God; What *is* with the Almighty I will not conceal" (Job 27:11 NKJV). Before he begins, however, he addresses the fact that his "students" are not ignorant; rather, have all seen it for themselves.[3] Job then closes out the chapter by continuing to speak regarding the "reward of the wicked."

---

1 See Job 27:2 NKJV
2 See Eph. 6:14
3 See Job 27:12a

Chapter Twenty-Three

JOB CHAPTER 28

IN SEARCH OF WEALTH

From the description of the future awaiting the wicked at the end of chapter 27, Job seems to take a bit of an aside in chapter 28. From verses 1-11, Job illustrates the lengths to which mankind will go in search of riches and great wealth. The effort mankind has expensed in order to "search the farthest recesses"[1] and explore the "hidden path" about which no bird of prey has even known.[2] Mankind really has not spared any effort in finding and grasping at the wealth God, in His provision, placed in the earth.

I wonder if Job has come to a similar conclusion as the writer of Ecclesiastes. Solomon found all of the wealth and status one can gain is, in the end, meaningless.³ Is Job realizing that he does not have all of the answers? Is he coming to the end of himself? Job, like Solomon, knew a life of luxury, great wealth and respect. Is he seeing how his past riches are of no help to him now? Is he seeing how the opinions and respect of man is actually fleeting? These questions arise as Job's thoughts turn now to the search for wisdom. Is Job learning what is found in Proverbs 4:7 NKJV; that "wisdom is the principal thing"?

IN SEARCH OF WISDOM

Job shows that wisdom cannot be bought with the finest of gold nor any precious jewel found in the earth.⁴ "But where can wisdom be found? And where *is* the place of understanding?" Job asks in Job 28:12 NKJV. The answer comes from Job in verse 23.

> ²³God understands its way,
> And He knows its place.
> ²⁴For He looks to the ends of the earth,
> *And* sees under the whole heavens,
> ²⁵To establish a weight for the wind,
> And apportion the waters by measure.
> ²⁶When He made a law for the rain,
> And a path for the thunderbolt,
> ²⁷Then He saw *wisdom* and declared it;
> He prepared it, indeed, He searched it out.
> ²⁸And to man He said, 'Behold, the fear of
> the Lord, that *is* wisdom, And to depart
> from evil *is* understanding.'" (Job 28:23-28 NKJV)

Such love is displayed when one realizes that something, which is worth more than mankind could possibly pay, is given freely to anyone willing to seek it out. It cannot be found by human means; it can only be found in God. Likewise, our salvation through Jesus is a free gift which man would not have the capacity for which to pay. First Corinthians 1:30 says that Jesus has become for us wisdom from God. This, as explained in the prior verses[5] was not based on high status but rather given to those who, in themselves, were defined as undeserving so that no one may boast before Him.

> Such love is displayed when one realizes that something, which is worth more than mankind could possibly pay, is given freely to anyone willing to seek it out.

Could it be that Job understands that, even if he had all of his riches back, it wouldn't be able to save him from the pain he is feeling? No amount of money could get his children back. No amount of respect from those at the city gate could restore Job's health. Job can truly see the benefits of seeking wisdom. Many of these benefits are seen in the Book of Proverbs.

---

1 See Job 28:3 NIV
2 See Job 28:7 NIV
3 See Eccl. 1:2
4 See Job 28:15-19
5 1 Cor. 1:26-29

Chapter Twenty-Four

JOB CHAPTER 29

MEMORY LANE

Chapter 29 sees Job continue his dialogue reminiscing about the not so distant past. It is interesting how Job recognizes the impact God had in his life.

²Oh, that I were as *in* months past, As *in* the days *when* God watched over me; ³When His lamp shone upon my head, *And when* by His light I walked *through* darkness; ⁴Just as I was in the days of my prime, When the friendly counsel of God *was* over my tent; ⁵When the Almighty *was* yet with me, *When* my

children *were* around me; ⁶When my steps were bathed with cream, And the rock poured out rivers of oil for me! (Job 29:2-6 NKJV)

Job reveals to us that he experienced an intimate friendship with God. This paints a picture of Job and God having a relationship in which Job would have known the most hidden details of God's character. Job would have had a deep revelation of exactly who God is and how He operates. That doesn't quite seem the case here. Looking at different translations and the original Hebrew word *sôd*, the term "intimate friendship" is more accurately shown as "counsel" or "secret counsel."[1] It is the same word Job used in Job 15:8a NKJV when he asked his companions, "Have you heard the counsel of God?" Again, the same Hebrew word is found in Proverbs 3:32 NKJV, "For the perverse *person* is an abomination to the LORD, But His secret counsel *is* with the upright."

Regardless of how close of a relationship Job had with God, we have confirmation here that Job had a relationship with God. Job received counsel from the Most High God! It is no surprise that Job had lived such a blessed life. So, what happened? In verse 5, Job reminisces about "when the Almighty was yet with [him]."[2] Since God said He would never leave us or forsake us,[3] this leaves but one option. Job must have "left" God. This is exactly what we discovered in the beginning chapters. Job left the hedge of protection. Job left the secret place of the Most High; that place where wisdom could be found. Job made himself vulnerable to attacks from the enemy. Without access to God's counsel, he did not know how to react. Job couldn't even recognize it as an enemy attack. He was in a place of ignorance rather than a place of wisdom.

Addressing Eliphaz' Accusations

In verse 7, Job gives the reader a glimpse of what his daily life was like just a short time before. He also gives response to Eliphaz who accused him in chapter 22.

Eliphaz Job 22 NKJV	Job Job 29 NKJV
- taken pledges from your brother for no reason (v. 6)	- broke fangs of the wicked (v. 17) - plucked the victim from his teeth (v. 17)
- stripped the naked of their clothing (v. 6)	- father to the poor (v. 16) - took up the case of the stranger[4] (v. 16)
- not given the weary water to drink (v. 7) - withheld bread from the hungry (v. 7) - crushed the strength of the fatherless (v. 9)	- rescued the poor who cried out, the fatherless and the one who had no helper[5] (v. 12)
- sent widows away empty (v. 9)	- caused the widow's heart to sing for joy (v. 13)
	- eyes for the blind (v. 15) - feet to the lame (v. 15)

One can see in the chart the variety of indictments with which Eliphaz accused Job. However, it looks here as though Job is fulfilling Isaiah 54:17a NKJV that declares, "No weapon formed against you shall prosper, And every tongue *which* rises against you in judgment You shall condemn." The New International Version says, "you will refute every tongue that accuses you."[6] Hopefully, as we continue, we'll see the first part of the verse realized as well where the weapon formed against Job will not prosper!

RESPECTED TO REJECTED

Job recollects how he had the respect of all men. People hung on his every word. Every word Job spoke to them fell gently on the listener's ears.[7] It is interesting how people drank in the "counsel" of Job. No doubt, much of the counsel of Job was a result of the counsel he had received from God. Job was likely receiving wisdom from God and bestowing it upon any who would listen. What happened when Job cut off the Source of that living word? He no longer had that word to pass along and the listeners closed their ears and opened their mouths against him.

While Job was living the good life, he thought the rest of his days would be just as good. Job's thoughts are expressed in verses 18-20.

> [18]"I thought, 'I will die in my own house, my days as numerous as the grains of sand. [19]My roots will reach to the water, and the dew will lie all night on my branches. [20]My glory will remain fresh in me, the bow ever new in my hand.'" (Job 29:18-20 NIV)

It was his own glory he thought would remain in him. Was Job so swept up in his good works and the pride associated with everyone having him up on a pedestal that he forgot about God? Did he think he was the one with the glory? Is that why he got himself outside of that precious secret place?

1 "H5475 - sôḏ - Strong's Hebrew Lexicon (nkjv)." Blue Letter Bible. Accessed 22 Oct, 2021.
https://www.blueletterbible.org/lexicon/h5475/nkjv/wlc/0-1/
2 Job 29:5 NKJV
3 Deut. 31:6, 8
4 See Job 29:16 NIV
5 See Job 29:12 NIV
6 Is. 54:17 NIV
7 Job 29:22 NIV

Chapter Twenty-Five

JOB CHAPTER 30

Perspective

Chapter 30 has Job describing how those who once admired him have turned against him. Then, in verse 11, Job has the audacity once again to blame God for his present circumstances. Even with ignorance of the behind the scenes, Job should at least be able to see his fault in not abiding with God in His secret place and in His counsel.

Job figures that God abandoned him and, because of this, it resulted in people abandoning him as well. People have now seen Job as vulnerable too. In verse 12, Job describes how people are now attacking and laying traps for him. It is evident that Satan is still doing his best to steal, kill and destroy with regard to Job.

CASE OF WELFARE

Still looking at his present circumstances, Job says in Job 30:15-17 NIV, "Terrors overwhelm me; my dignity is driven away as by the wind, my safety vanishes like a cloud. And now my life ebbs away; days of suffering grip me. Night pierces my bones; my gnawing pains never rest." It is interesting that the Hebrew word used in verse 15 for "safety" is actually the word "yeshua."[1] We best know this word as referring to Jesus. In Hebrew, it means, "salvation, deliverance, welfare, prosperity and victory."[2]
Gesenius' Hebrew-Chaldee Lexicon attributes "welfare" as the appropriate usage of this word in Job 30:15.[3] That being said, Job is stating that his welfare is vanishing like a cloud or storm. What a sad reality; to believe that your source of salvation is vanishing. Perhaps Job's hope in being able to save himself was vanishing but the true Source of salvation was always available and at the ready. The Shelter and Secret Place of the Most High was still present and prepared for Job's return.

UNSEEN EVIDENCE

Job has descended even deeper into the place of woe and torment. He describes the suffering he continues to endure. The saddest part, however, is perhaps Job's belief that God has turned His back on Job. In verse 20, Job says that he has cried out to God but that his pleas have gone unanswered. How familiar is this today? So many have been in a similar situation where they cannot find any evidence that God is answering their prayers. Just because we cannot see something, though, doesn't mean it's not there. Hebrews 11:1 NKJV states, "Now faith is the substance of things hoped for; the evidence of things not seen." Anyone who has planted a seed in the ground knows that the seed is growing before any sign of a sprout appears above the dirt. God is at work when we pray. Sometimes, however, it takes time for our physical senses to see, feel, smell, taste or hear any evidence of it. This is when it is doubly helpful to know God is love. A loving God cares and does help those who trust in Him.

There are instances, too, when we do not hear God's response to us because we are too busy listening to others or even to ourselves. In Job's case, he says that God didn't answer him. Did Job ever stop talking long enough for God to have an opportunity to reply? Love is patient.[4] God is patient. Love is not rude.[5] God is not rude. God will wait until we are finished and ready to listen.

---

1 "H3444 - yᵉšûʿâ - Strong's Hebrew Lexicon (niv)." Blue Letter Bible. Accessed 22 Oct, 2021.
https://www.blueletterbible.org/lexicon/h3444/niv/wlc/0-1/
2 "H3444 - yᵉšûʿâ - Strong's Hebrew Lexicon (niv)." Blue Letter Bible. Accessed 22 Oct, 2021.
https://www.blueletterbible.org/lexicon/h3444/niv/wlc/0-1/
3 "H3444 - yᵉšûʿâ – Gesenius' Hebrew-Chaldee Lexicon (niv)." Blue Letter Bible. Accessed 22 Oct, 2021.
https://www.blueletterbible.org/lexicon/h3444/niv/wlc/0-1/
4 See 1 Cor. 13:4 RSV
5 See 1 Cor. 13:5 RSV

Chapter Twenty-Six

JOB CHAPTER 31

FIVE STAGES

As with the five stages of grief, Job has developed in his stages throughout this time of torment. He has gone through **denial** that he has done anything wrong. He has maintained his position of being upright and blameless. Job has a solid foundation in his thinking here as God Himself called it so. However, Job did not recognize his part in making himself vulnerable and open to attack.

Job has been in the stage of **anger** where he is angry at his circumstances, his comforters and God for all that has happened to him and their response or presumed lack thereof.

Job Chapter 31

Job has gone through **bargaining** where he recounts to his listeners and to God all of the golden checkmarks he has produced throughout his life. If restored, undoubtedly he would continue to do good deeds and be the ultimate philanthropist.

The stage of **depression** seems to be a constant for Job. From the beginning chapters until even now Job speaks from the position of a despairing man.

Chapter 31 seems to be where Job comes to an **acceptance** stage. Many "ifs" are mentioned in chapter 31. It is as though Job has come to the place where he concedes that "if" he has done anything to deserve the horrible happenings that have come upon him, he will accept them. "If" he is in fact guilty, he will accept the punishment due him. I do not think Job believed that he had committed any offence or had left any sin without an appropriate offering. It is, instead, Job's position that if there was anything he had done wrong or not done right and was ignorant of such occurrences that he would understand why a Righteous Judge would then give a guilty verdict.

STEP TRACKER

Job knows that God sees his ways and counts his steps.[1] He shows throughout chapter 31 his reverence for God and His ways. He also shows his fear of God by admitting, "For I dreaded destruction from God, and for fear of His splendor I could not do such things" (Job 31:23 NIV). Job had such an awareness of God's ways and the consequences of both walking in and straying from them. Job knew he should be honest,[2] be faithful in marriage,[3] walk justly in business,[4] be generous to those in need,[5]

> A loving God is focused on love and set love as the standard by which to live.

put his trust in God and not in riches,[6] put God first above all,[7] and keep his words pure.[8] Many of these ways of life can also be seen in the Ten Commandments. They can be summed up in like manner, to what Jesus declared in Matthew 22:37-40 when He said that all of the law and prophets hang on loving God and loving others. A loving God is focused on love and set love as the standard by which to live.

JOB RESTS HIS CASE

As his remarks come to a close it is as if the court now hears, "the defense rests its case." Job 31:35 NIV proclaims, "Oh that I had someone to hear me! I sign now my defense – let the Almighty answer me; let my accuser put his indictment in writing." And, with what seems appropriate timing to play Handel's "Hallelujah Chorus" in the background, Job 31:40b NKJV states, "The words of Job are ended." Someone please join in my celebration! Job finally stops speaking!

---

1 Job 31:4
2 See Job 31:5
3 See Job 31:9
4 See Job 31:13
5 See Job 31:16-21
6 See Job 31:24, 25
7 See Job 31:27, 28
8 See Job 31:30

Chapter Twenty-Seven

JOB CHAPTER 32

ELIHU

Not only does Job stop speaking, but verse 1 of chapter 32 tells us that the three other men stopped as well. But wait! What do we find out? We find out now that there weren't only three men in Job's midst all this time. Similar to the story of the fiery furnace, there was a fourth man there all along![1] Elihu son of Barakel the Buzite, of the family of Ram is now introduced to the reader.

The Hebrew meanings behind these names help to give a more detailed look into Elihu. Elihu is from the family of Ram. In Hebrew, "Ram" means "high" or "exalted."[2] His father's name, "Barakel" is translated as, "God blesses."[3] "Elihu" means, "He is my God."[4]

So far we can see the description of a man who comes from a high and exalted family, with "God blesses" as the father and who himself is the son who says, "He is my God." This could sound as one who is setting out to describe Jesus! Jesus comes from a highly exalted family where His Father blesses. Jesus can also be seen foreshadowed in the ram in Genesis 22:13 with the account of Abraham and Isaac.

The place that makes one scratch their head is the meaning of the word "Buzite." It could simply mean, "a descendent of Buz," but, in Hebrew, it is also translated as "contempt."[5] Contempt? How could that possibly fit amongst the other descriptors? *Webster's Dictionary 1828* gives the following definition for the word "contempt":

> The act of despising; the act of viewing or considering and treating as mean, vile and worthless; disdain, hatred of what is mean or deemed vile. This word is one of the strongest expressions of a mean opinion which the language affords.[6]

Elihu does seem angry with Job and the other three; but contempt? Jesus was put in the category of being despised but does that really fit here? It is not until one sees a deeper insight into that which Elihu represents that the word contempt really fits.

GRACE REVEALED

Looking back, we see that the three companions have represented "tradition," "legalism" and "self-effort." What could show contempt toward such things? Only grace. Elihu represents grace. Grace is undeserved and unearned favor. In scripture, it is often found related to the number 5. If one counts Job and his three companions, Elihu is shown as the fifth man in the group. Grace will always "butt heads" with the Law. This is because whenever the Law is mixed with grace, it is no longer grace. As soon as an element of self-effort or "earning" is introduced, it can no longer be counted as grace. It would be the same if it were required that someone give money to the clerk at the store to buy a free gift. As soon as the smallest amount is paid, it is no longer free.

This contempt can be seen in Elihu's reaction. Verse 2 and 3 both mention how angry Elihu was toward Job and the three others. He was angry with Job "because he justified himself rather than God" (Job 32:2b NKJV). The Hebrew word ṣāḏaq describes Job as having declared himself just or innocent.[7] Job, while he had asked for his day in court, basically rendered his own verdict. At the same time as calling himself "not guilty," he also called God "guilty" of being unjust.

Elihu's anger burned against the three companions "because they had found no answer, and *yet* had condemned Job" (Job 32:3 NKJV). Again, the Hebrew gives a bit more insight into the language used. It shows the friends could find no "contradiction" or "refutation" for Job.[8] "Refutation" can be defined as follows:

> The act or process of refuting or disproving; the act of proving to be false or erroneous; the overthrowing of an argument, opinion, testimony, doctrine or theory, by argument or countervailing proof.[9]

The friends could not disprove Job's innocence and yet they declared him guilty. Interestingly, the New International Version gives a footnote saying, "Job, and so had condemned God" as the ending of verse three.[10] Could it be in not being able to disprove Job's innocence claim, they inadvertently implied God was guilty of being unjust? Isn't this how arguments of "tradition," "legalism" and "self-effort" often conclude?

"Now because they *were* years older than he, Elihu had waited to speak to Job" (Job 32:4 NKJV). Elihu waited. Elihu was, as the Word directs in James 1:19 NIV, "quick to listen, slow to speak and slow to become angry." It must have taken great restraint for Elihu to remain silent while the others carried on as they did. Did Elihu's silence "speak"? Did the four even notice Elihu was there? Did they see him as he silently endured their speeches? Do legalism, tradition and self-effort even recognize grace in their midst? How many people are distracted from even seeing the presence of grace when the voices of legalism, tradition and self-effort are so loud around them? We must make an effort to see and hear the grace that is ever-present and at-the-ready even when contrary voices are demanding our attention and desperately trying to be heard.

It was because the others were older that Elihu waited. God's grace is evident even before the giving of the Law. Why would grace be considered "younger"? I believe it is because the grace message, which came to tell people that they could receive salvation through receiving Jesus and all He did for us, is "newer" than the righteousness through faith and deeds found in the Old Testament. The message Paul preached was radical to the hearers of his day. Elihu was there the entire time. If we broaden our view in looking at scripture, we can likewise see that Grace was there the entire time. Like in Job, Grace simply wasn't recognized until later on.

Looking at Elihu himself, however, he was younger than the four others. He showed them respect in waiting his turn. One can see the expectation Elihu had though. He expected the others to speak with wisdom. Surely, throughout their many years they had acquired wisdom. It is easy to see Elihu's disappointment when wisdom was not found in the abundance of their speech. Elihu learned as he indicated in Job 32:8 NKJV, "But *there is* a spirit in man, And the breath of the Almighty gives him understanding." Wisdom comes from God and, as seen in James 1:5, God will give wisdom generously to anyone who asks. Anyone who asks for wisdom will receive it; anyone who seeks for wisdom will find it. [11] Similarly, to Elihu, God sent Jeremiah and Timothy to speak. Jeremiah and Timothy were also youths.

> But the LORD said to me:" Do not say, 'I *am* a youth,' For you shall go to all to whom I send you, And whatever I command you, you shall speak. (Jer. 1:7 NKJV)

> Let no one despise your youth, but be an example to the believers in word, in conduct, in love, in spirit, in faith, in purity. (1 Tim. 4:12 NKJV)

It should be an encouragement to all that God is able to use anyone He chooses regardless of age to speak His Word and proclaim His Kingdom!

God is also able to give discernment to his people. The word translated as "understanding" in verse 8 means "to know what is right."[12] Elihu was able to discern what opinion concerning Job was right. He certainly knew that what the four had said was not right.

Elihu sees that the three comforters are now silent. He describes their current state in Job 32:15 NKJV, "They are dismayed and answer no more; Words escape them." The word "dismayed" is interesting; it is translated as "shattered" and "broken."[13] This describes their state well. The positions of legalism, tradition and self-effort are broken. They are not able or equipped to save anyone.

READY TO BURST

I can feel the compulsion within Elihu as he lets loose all that he has been holding back.

> [18]For I am full of words; The spirit within me compels me. [19]Indeed my belly *is* like wine *that* has no vent; It is ready to burst like new wineskins. [20]I will speak, that I may find relief; I must open my lips and answer. (Job 32:18-20 NKJV)

Let all restraints be loosened! Let's hear what Grace has to say!

"I will show partiality to no one, nor will I flatter any man" (Job 32:21 NIV). Grace shows no partiality. Acts 10:34b NKJV says, "In truth I perceive that God shows no partiality." Additionally, Grace will not flatter any man because Grace knows that man can do nothing of himself to save anyone. I suppose this is why, in verse 22, it says that if he were to flatter anyone, God would take him away. If Grace all of a sudden were to "flatter" someone by telling them they are able to save themselves apart from God, there would be no place for Grace any longer. It is only through the gift of Grace given to us by God that anyone can be saved.

> It should be an encouragement to all that God is able to use anyone He chooses regardless of age to speak His Word and proclaim His Kingdom!

1 See Daniel 3
2 "H7410 - rām - Strong's Hebrew Lexicon (nkjv)." Blue Letter Bible. Accessed 23 Oct, 2021.
https://www.blueletterbible.org/lexicon/h7410/nkjv/wlc/0-1/
3 "H1292 - bāraḵ'ēl - Strong's Hebrew Lexicon (nkjv)." Blue Letter Bible. Accessed 23 Oct, 2021.
https://www.blueletterbible.org/lexicon/h1292/nkjv/wlc/0-1/
4 "H453 - 'ĕlîhû - Strong's Hebrew Lexicon (nkjv)." Blue Letter Bible. Accessed 23 Oct, 2021.
https://www.blueletterbible.org/lexicon/h453/nkjv/wlc/0-1/
5 "H940 - bûzî - Strong's Hebrew Lexicon (nkjv)." Blue Letter Bible. Accessed 23 Oct, 2021.
https://www.blueletterbible.org/lexicon/h940/nkjv/wlc/0-1/
6 Webster, Noah. "Contempt." Webster's Dictionary 1828, 23 Oct. 2021, http://www.webstersdictionary1828.com/Dictionary/contempt. Accessed 23 Oct. 2021.
7 "H6663 - ṣāḏaq – Gesenius' Hebrew-Chaldee Lexicon (nkjv)." Blue Letter Bible. Accessed 23 Oct, 2021.
https://www.blueletterbible.org/lexicon/h6663/nkjv/wlc/0-1/
8 "H4617 - maʿănê – Gesenius' Hebrew-Chaldee Lexicon (nkjv)." Blue Letter Bible. Accessed 23 Oct, 2021.
https://www.blueletterbible.org/lexicon/h4617/nkjv/wlc/0-1/
9 Webster, Noah. "Refutation." Webster's Dictionary 1828, 23 Oct. 2021, http://www.webstersdictionary1828.com/Dictionary/refutation. Accessed 23 Oct. 2021.
10 "Job 32 (NIV) - He was also angry with." Blue Letter Bible. Accessed 23 Oct, 2021.
https://www.blueletterbible.org/niv/job/32/3/s_468003
11 See Matt. 7:7
12 "H995 - bîn – Gesenius' Hebrew-Chaldee Lexicon (nkjv)." Blue Letter Bible. Accessed 24 Oct, 2021.
https://www.blueletterbible.org/lexicon/h995/nkjv/wlc/0-1/
13 "H2865 - ḥāṯaṯ - Strong's Hebrew Lexicon (nkjv)." Blue Letter Bible. Accessed 24 Oct, 2021.
https://www.blueletterbible.org/lexicon/h2865/nkjv/wlc/0-1/

Chapter Twenty-Eight

JOB CHAPTER 33

ELIHU CONTINUES

In chapter 33, Elihu continues speaking to Job. It is interesting to note that Elihu is not addressing the other three. Job has been the one seeking answers and Elihu is ready to respond to his search. Elihu, according to verse 3, speaks sincerely from an upright heart. His list of qualifications is not heavy with education or years of study, it is simply that, "The Spirit of God has made me; the breath of the Almighty gives me life" (Job 33:4 NIV). This is the same source given in Job 32:8 for Elihu's understanding and discretion.

Elihu gives an example of what Job has been saying in the previous chapters.

> [8]"Surely you have spoken in my hearing, And I have heard the sound of *your* words, *saying,* [9]'I *am* pure, without transgression; I *am* innocent, and *there is* no iniquity in me. [10]Yet He finds occasions against me, He counts me as His enemy; [11]He puts my feet in the stocks, He watches all my paths.' (Job 33:8-11 NKJV)

Looking at verse 9, it is a far contrast to Job's true position of being "upright and blameless" as God described at the beginning of the Book of Job. Job apparently has now claimed to be without sin. Perhaps Job sees it this way because he believes he offered sacrifices for every sin he had ever done. Even if this were the case, and the sacrifices he did had covered over every sin, the verses that followed are easily seen as "not right." Job 33:12a NKJV shows Elihu confirming this, "Look, *in* this you are not righteous." "Righteous," in this instance, refers to speaking the truth or what is right.[1] God did not do what Job alleges in verses 10 and 11.

Elihu proceeds to tell Job what he knows about God. He lets Job know that God, in fact, does, speak to man. If man does not hear God speak, it could be that man is simply not discerning it. "Why do you complain to him that he responds to no one's words? For God does speak—now one way, now another—though no one perceives it." (Job 33:13, 14 NIV). God, Elihu explains, may speak to men in visions and dreams. He even cares enough to warn people in visions and dreams to keep them from destructive behavior. In this, you can see God's love at its root.

DEPICTION

Verses 19–22 depict a man on the brink of death. This is a picture of someone who is experiencing spiritual death too. It is what would happen if there was no Mediator. Just such a Mediator is described in the verses that follow. Leave it to Elihu to present Job with the Grace Message!

"Well, all that you've laid out in this book has been all well and good up until now but how do you explain verses 19-21? It looks as though this loving God has made this man sick to teach him something." I imagine someone somewhere with such a statement. Firstly, it does not say that God made this person sick; it merely states his dismal condition. Secondly, I believe these verses are painting a picture of mankind's spiritual condition through the fall. The word, "chastened" in verse 19 is translated as a passive tense of "to correct by punishment, to punish."[2] As Romans 5:12 explains, death came to all mankind through Adam's sin. Romans 6:23 explains further that, "the wages of sin is death."

FOOD FOR THOUGHT

Digging even deeper, let's look at the food mentioned in verse 20. The "food" this man finds repulsive is the Hebrew word *leḥem*.[3] The first reference of this word in scripture is from Genesis 3:19. It speaks of the bread gained by the hard labor that came from the curse of the fall. The "choicest meal" his soul loathes comes from the word *ma'ăkāl*.[4] The first reference of this word is found in Genesis 2:9 in describing the fruit of the trees God provided in the Garden of Eden. So, it can be reasoned that this man finds the working of his own self-effort repulsive and his soul loathes the goodness provided by God. What a struggle this person is in! It is clear by verses 21 and 22 that this person is dying. Even if this were to speak of a physical man in such a despairing condition, it is not a condition given by God. It would not be God's will that anyone be in such a condition – spiritually or physically. This is why God sent Jesus to endure the stripes by which we are healed.[5] It is sometimes, however, only when someone is in such a desperate time, when they finally decide to call on God for help.

FLESH AND BONE

One can see the theme of self-effort hidden in Job 33:21 NKJV as well, "His flesh wastes away from sight, And his bones stick out *which once* were not seen."

Flesh can often be linked to self-effort. This man could be considered to be in a position where he is no longer able to help himself. His self-effort is no longer effectual; its ability to save has ended. The bone can represent "firmness" or "strength."[6] This points to the man's strength to save himself. The Hebrew word *šāpâ* is shown to mean, "His bones become naked of flesh."[7] In other words, his internal strength, which has been previously unseen, has also been shown to be stripped of all self-effort. Clearly this person has, up to this point, been unsuccessful in saving himself. God is always eager to help anyone who seeks Him. This is a man who has been trying to go it alone. Mankind is unable to save itself. Eventually, it is discovered and proven that man's own strength and self-effort is inadequate in this area. The sin introduced to mankind through the fall, results in curse and death. Verse 22 shows how the man is heading toward death.

IN NEED OF A MEDIATOR AND RANSOM

Thankfully, God did not leave mankind to such a fate. The blessed message of grace shines through in the verses that follow. "If there is a messenger for him, A mediator, one among a thousand, To show man His uprightness, Then He is gracious to him, and says, 'Deliver him from going down to the Pit; I have found a ransom' (Job 33:23, 24 NKJV). The grace message is here saying that if someone would come and explain to a person how they are to be made right with God[8] (only through receiving Jesus and what He did for us), God will show him grace and he will be delivered and set free from eternal death. The reason: a ransom was found. Jesus was that ransom and can be found in Matthew 20:28, Mark 10:45, First Timothy 2:6 and Titus 2:14.

What is the result? Job33:25 NKJV says, "His flesh shall be young like a child's, He shall return to the days of his youth." What?! Is the self-effort restored? No, on the contrary, a child is dependent on his parents. The flesh will be as in the days of his youth. This is a state of humility where one is dependent on the Father. This is also an amazing healing scripture. God is also able to raise up those on sickbeds and deathbeds and restore them to their youthful vigor.

The Ransom has been found. Now, in humility (knowing you need the Ransom), the person is able to pray to God and find favour with Him. "He shall pray to God, and He will delight in him, He shall see His face with joy, For He restores to man His righteousness" (Job 33:26 NKJV). Oh! How glorious! Once the man realizes his need for a Savior, all he needs to do is receive Him. Immediately, God restores the man to the righteous state he had before the fall. He is now the righteousness of God in Christ Jesus taught about in scripture.

> [22]But now the righteousness of God apart from the law is revealed, being witnessed by the Law and the Prophets, [23]even the righteousness of God, through faith in Jesus Christ, to all and on all who believe. For there is no difference; (Rom. 3:21, 22 NKJV)

> ²¹For He made Him who knew no sin *to be* sin for us, that we might become the righteousness of God in Him.
> (2 Cor. 5:21 NKJV)

The Young's Literal Translation puts it this way: "He maketh supplication unto God, And He accepteth him. And he seeth His face with shouting, And He returneth to man His righteousness" (Job 33:26 YLT).

What happens next? The man tells the news of the mercy and grace God has shown. "And they will go to others and say, 'I have sinned, I have perverted what is right, but I did not get what I deserved. God has delivered me from going down to the pit, and I shall live to enjoy the light of life" (Job 33:27, 28 NIV).

Job 33:29, 30 NLT show the length God is willing to go to save a man and all mankind, "Yes, God does these things again and again for people. He rescues them from the grave so they may enjoy the light of life."

It would be good for Job to take Elihu's advice and "pay attention."[9]

---

1 "H6663 - ṣāḏaq – Gesenius' Hebrew-Chaldee Lexicon (nkjv)." Blue Letter Bible. Accessed 18 Jan, 2023.
https://www.blueletterbible.org/lexicon/h6663/nkjv/wlc/0-1/
2 "H3198 - yāḵaḥ - Gesenius' Hebrew-Chaldee Lexicon (nkjv)." Blue Letter Bible. Accessed 24 Oct, 2021.
https://www.blueletterbible.org/lexicon/h3198/nkjv/wlc/0-1/
3 "H3899 - leḥem - Strong's Hebrew Lexicon (nkjv)." Blue Letter Bible. Accessed 24 Oct, 2021.
https://www.blueletterbible.org/lexicon/h3899/nkjv/wlc/0-1/
4 "H3978 - ma'ăḵāl - Strong's Hebrew Lexicon (nkjv)." Blue Letter Bible. Accessed 24 Oct, 2021.
https://www.blueletterbible.org/lexicon/h3978/nkjv/wlc/0-1/
5 See Is. 53:5 NKJV
6 "H6106 - ʿeṣem – Gesenius' Hebrew-Chaldee Lexicon (nkjv)." Blue Letter Bible. Accessed 25 Oct, 2021.
https://www.blueletterbible.org/lexicon/h6106/nkjv/wlc/0-1/

7 "H8192 - šāpā – Gesenius' Hebrew-Chaldee Lexicon (nkjv)." Blue Letter Bible. Accessed 25 Oct, 2021. https://www.blueletterbible.org/lexicon/h8192/nkjv/wlc/0-1/
8 See Job 33:23 Amplified Bible
9 See Job 33:31 NIV

Chapter Twenty-Nine

JOB CHAPTER 34

EVIDENCE EXAMINED

Once the clear grace message was presented, Elihu directed his speech toward all of the wise men within his hearing. He seems to encourage the wise among him to examine the evidence and conclude what is correct.

> ³For the ear tests words as the tongue tastes food. ⁴Let us discern for ourselves what is right; let us learn together what is good. (Job 34:3, 4 NIV)

Elihu presents exhibit one: Job's words. "For Job has said, 'I am righteous, But God has taken away my justice; Should I lie concerning my right? My wound *is* incurable, *though I am* without transgression'" (Job 34:5, 6 NKJV). Exhibit two: "He keeps company with evildoers; he associates with the wicked. For he says, 'There is no profit in trying to please God'" (Job 34:8, 9 NIV). There is a theme here where it shows Job's attitude; an inaccurate view of who God really is.

In God's defense, Elihu reminds the listeners that God is just and it is even "unthinkable that God would do wrong."[1] He continues to remind them that God is above everything including the very breath in our lungs. God Almighty knows all and nothing is hidden from Him. The people who choose to turn away from God no longer live with His protection or blessing. They reap from what they have sown.

The wise men conclude, it seems, that "Job speaks without knowledge, His words *are* without wisdom."[2] Elihu hopes that Job will be tried to the utmost for speaking as he has. The word "tried" here is the same used in verse 3; it is a hope that Job will be examined fully.[3] Elihu finishes the chapter saying, "For you have added rebellion to your sin; you show no respect, and you speak many angry words against God" (Job 34:37 NLT).

---

1 Job 34:12a NIV
2 Job 34:35 NKJV
3 "H974 - bāḥan - Strong's Hebrew Lexicon (nkjv)." Blue Letter Bible. Accessed 25 Oct, 2021.
https://www.blueletterbible.org/lexicon/h974/nkjv/wlc/0-1/

Chapter Thirty

JOB CHAPTER 35

QUESTIONS OF RIGHTEOUSNESS

Elihu questions Job at the beginning of the chapter probing, "Do you think this is right? Do you say, 'My righteousness is more than God's'?" (Job 35:2 NKJV). It certainly looks as though Elihu is more than implying that Job is looking at his own righteousness as being superior to God's. We have seen Job endeavoring to maintain righteousness through his own strivings. Trying to maintain one's own righteousness is akin to haughtily telling God that there is no need for the righteousness He has provided. Some older versions of the New International Version[1] quotes Job 35:2b as saying, "You say, 'I will be cleared by God.'" This appears to show Job perceiving his "innocence" despite the accusations all while confidently knowing that God will vindicate him with a "not guilty" verdict.

In either instance, Job goes on to ask (according to Elihu) what Job will gain by living uprightly and not sinning. Because Job is still in the midst of his circumstances, he has wondered what the benefit of being upright and blameless could possibly be if he, in the end, has received the same result as one who has lived wickedly. It would be very easy to question "the system" when focusing on self in the difficult moments.

Unchanging

Now, Elihu moves to address Job and his companions. Elihu draws their attention heavenward asking them how their sin affects God. Their level of righteousness or unrighteousness does not change God. God is still Love, God is still righteous, and God is still omnipotent and omnipresent. He is still above all. Likewise, if we accuse God, it does not change or affect who He is.

"Your wickedness only affects humans like yourself, and your righteousness only other people" (Job 35:8 NIV). Elihu continues to say how people will cry out under oppression but seem to forget to ask God for help.[2] They neglect to remember God is their Maker and all that He has given to mankind. He gives us songs of joy and triumph in the midst of adversity[3] and gives mankind more wisdom and learning than other creatures He has made.[4] And, because of man's pride and arrogance in crying out to anyone but God, He does not answer.[5] Surely, if anyone were to sincerely call on God for help, He would hear them and help them.

It is an "empty plea" God does not regard;[6] not the sincere cries of people. So, Elihu concludes, if God is paying no attention to empty pleas, why would

He concern Himself with listening to empty and baseless complaints and accusations. Elihu confirms once again that, "Job opens his mouth with empty talk; without knowledge he multiplies words" (Job 35: 16 NIV).

UNCHANGING LOVE

With all of this, there is an undertone of God is love. Even though it is said here that God is uninterested in the cries of the arrogant, He still cares about everyone. Even though Job and his companions may have missed the mark in many ways, God still put Elihu in their midst to try to get their thinking moved in the right direction. The sin of mankind does not change God but His love for all His creation did move Him to action. God acted before the foundation of the world.[7] He acted before man ever sinned. He desires a relationship with us and made sure that was made possible through Jesus.

---

1 The NIV/KJV Parallel Bible, (Grand Rapids, MI, Zondervan, 2002), 886.
2 See Job 35:9, 10
3 "H2158 - zᵉmir – Gesenius' Hebrew-Chaldee Lexicon (niv)." Blue Letter Bible. Accessed 25 Oct, 2021.
https://www.blueletterbible.org/lexicon/h2158/niv/wlc/0-1/
4 See Job 35:10, 11
5 See Job 35:12
6 See Job 35:13 NIV
7 See Rev. 13:8 NKJV

Chapter Thirty-One

JOB CHAPTER 36

SPEAKING ON GOD'S BEHALF

Elihu asks that the four have some patience with him as he continues.[1] It begs the question as to whether they were impatient or agitated by what they were hearing. The feathers of tradition, experience and self-effort do often get somewhat ruffled in response to grace. Nevertheless, Elihu presses on because he has more to say on God's behalf. What is Elihu's first declaration he says on behalf of God? Elihu confirms God's justice and righteousness.[2] The Hebrew word used for righteousness in verse 3 also includes justice as part of its definition.[3]

At first glance, verse four makes Elihu appear quite full of himself. "For truly my words *are* not false; One who is perfect in knowledge *is* with you." (Job 36:4 NKJV). The Hebrew words translated into "perfect" and "knowledge" show the deeper roots of "perfect, complete, whole" [4] and "knowledge of God"[5] respectively. If one looks, once again, as Elihu representing grace, it seems to make more sense. Grace would ascribe righteousness and justice to God. That is why grace was needed; because man was unable to satisfy the righteous requirements on his own. Additionally, grace would be perfect and complete in the knowledge of God.

Elihu continues to address the allegations given by Job concerning God. Contrary to what Job had said in pervious chapters, God does not despise or reject people and He does not prolong the lives of the wicked. Instead, God is "mighty in power and heart" (Job 36:5 YLT) and, as confirmed in Psalms 103:8 NKJV, "The LORD *is* merciful and gracious, Slow to anger, and abounding in mercy."

CHOICES

But, Elihu continues, if someone is experiencing affliction, God will shine a light as to why.[6] Note that God is not the source of the affliction. It is, according to verse 9, the result of their own doing. Does God leave them to the calamitous consequences? No! It is quite the opposite! "He also opens their ear to instruction, And commands that they turn from iniquity" (Job 36:10 NKJV). Then, just as God set before the Israelites the choice between life and death and blessings and curses in Deuteronomy 30:19, God sets out a choice in Job 36:11, 12 NKJV, "If they obey and serve *Him,* They shall spend their days in prosperity, And their years in pleasures. But if they do not obey, They shall perish by the sword, And they shall die without knowledge."

God, in His love, will do what He can to bring deliverance. Sometimes it is only when someone is suffering that they will seek deliverance. In many cases, the suffering and affliction could have been avoided had they just sought God sooner.

Elihu tells Job that God is indeed beckoning for him to return to His Secret Place. "Indeed He would have brought you out of dire distress, *Into* a broad place where *there is* no restraint; And what is set on your table *would be* full of richness" (Job 36:16 NKJV). In other words, "therefore choose life" (Deut. 30:19b NKJV).

WARNINGS

Next, Elihu brings some warnings to Job. He seems to point out the dangers of the direction in which Job is headed. "But you are filled with the judgment due the wicked; Judgment and justice take hold *of you*. Because *there is* wrath, *beware* lest He take you away with *one* blow; For a large ransom would not help you avoid *it*" (Job 36:17, 18 NKJV). This brings to mind the warning in Matthew 7:1, 2 NKJV, "Judge not, that you be not judged. For with what judgment you judge, you will be judged; and with the measure you use, it will be measured back to you." It is as though Elihu is cautioning Job to stop standing in judgement. Job has begun to compare the circumstances of others based on his perception of their level of wickedness. Elihu continues to admonish Job not to enter into mockery of the judicial system because, if he were to mock God's judgements, he might inadvertently end up rejecting the ransom given by God.[7] If Job were to deem himself more righteous than others and conclude that God's judicial system is unjust and flawed, Job might enter into territory where he maintains standing on his own righteousness. This would leave no room for the Ransom given through grace.

Verse 19 seems to warn Job not to trust in his own strength or wealth to save him. God's favor cannot be bought. He already has all of the gold and power He wants and needs. Yet another caution is found in Job 36:20 NKJV to, "not desire the night, When people are cut off in their place." How many times did we see Job longing for just that? Lastly, Elihu's final warning comes when he says to Job, "Take heed, do not turn to iniquity, For you have chosen this rather than affliction" (Job 36:21 NKJV). Do not be fooled, Job, into thinking the wicked seems to be living the good life while you, in your uprightness, are reaping adversity. The circumstances you are in are an attack and not a result of an unjust verdict. Don't fall for the lie of, "If I can't beat 'em, I'll join 'em."

COMPARING PSALM 107

Elihu then continues to relate to Job how much farther God's ways are above our ways. He calls on Job to behold and remember how exalted God and the work of His hands truly are.

There is a comparison to be made between this chapter and Psalm 107. Psalm 107 shows a few examples of how, in people's dire circumstances, the people call out to God. Some of these circumstances are the result of being lost and wandering in a wilderness experience, some have dissented against the words and counsel of God. Others are in this condition due to rebellious ways and sin. Some others were in the midst of a storm. Regardless of what got them into a place of desperation, God was faithful to answer their various calls for help. The Psalm reminds us to recognize the LORD's unfailing love. Verse 2 confirms those who were redeemed of the LORD, had been redeemed from the hand of the enemy.

---

1 See Job 36:2
2 See Job 36:3 NKJV
3 "H6664 - ṣeḏeq - Strong's Hebrew Lexicon (nkjv)." Blue Letter Bible. Accessed 25 Oct, 2021.
https://www.blueletterbible.org/lexicon/h6664/nkjv/wlc/0-1/

4 "H8549 - tāmîm - Strong's Hebrew Lexicon (nkjv)." Blue Letter Bible. Accessed 25 Oct, 2021.
https://www.blueletterbible.org/lexicon/h8549/nkjv/wlc/0-1/
5 "H1844 - dēʿâ - Strong's Hebrew Lexicon (nkjv)." Blue Letter Bible. Accessed 25 Oct, 2021.
https://www.blueletterbible.org/lexicon/h1844/nkjv/wlc/0-1/
6 See Job 36:9
7 See Job 36:18

Chapter Thirty-Two

JOB CHAPTER 37

THUNDER AND LIGHTNING

Elihu continues to expound on the nature and character of God in chapter 37. There is much talk of God's thunder and lightning. It is only upon digging deeper that one finds more insight into that of which Elihu speaks. There are a few different Hebrew words used when translating "thunder," "thundereth," etc. The word *ra'am* speaks of a peal of thunder.[1] The word *qôl*, however, speaks more of a voice or a sound.[2] This is the same word used when, in Genesis 3:8, Adam and Eve heard the sound of God in the Garden of Eden.

Normally, in the Old Testament, thunder showed a sign of God's power and majesty, showed a sign that the Earth is His[3] as well as a showing of God's judgement. As stated before, judgement has two sides. A person who is judged can be found guilty or not guilty. A storm with thunder can bring a flood but could also bring water that causes the crops to grow abundantly.

At any rate, verse one shows that Elihu's heart is both trembling and leaping with anticipation of what is coming. He implores those in his midst to listen! Such excellent advice! Listen to what God is saying and is about to say! Verse 3 shares in the excitement that the voice of God is let loose throughout the entire earth. It says that God's lightning, too, goes to the ends of the earth. The word for lightning can also be translated as "light."[4] In fact, it is first used in Genesis 1:3 NKJV when God said, "Let there be light."

Not only is God's voice going throughout the earth, He is also sending light to the ends of the earth. Job 37:4, in fact, shows that the lightning is unleashed and then, after that, comes the sound of His roar. Just like in nature, one sees the flashes of lightning before one hears the peal of thunder. In actuality, however, both happen at the same time. It is the distinction between the speed of light and the speed of sound that makes the perceived difference. Likewise, Jesus is both the Light of the World and the Word of God. Both were together in the Beginning and both came to the earth together in the person of Jesus. People often need the Light to shine before they can receive the Word. The Light helps to expose what has been in darkness. I love how it says in verse 4 that God holds nothing back when His voice is heard. "God thunders marvelously with His voice; He does great things which we cannot comprehend" (Job 37:5 NKJV).

Job Chapter 37

THE RAIN

Such mercy God shows in watering the earth with both snow and rain. A loving God made sure that snowflakes fall with such gentleness even though coming from such a great height. Matthew 5:44, 45 links God's love as well to the rain He sends to the earth.

> ⁴⁴But I say to you, love your enemies, bless those who curse you, do good to those who hate you, and pray for those who spitefully use you and persecute you, ⁴⁵that you may be sons of your Father in heaven; for He makes His sun rise on the evil and on the good, and sends rain on the just and on the unjust. (Matt. 5:44, 45 NKJV)

REST

Likewise Job 37:7 NKJV shows God's love for His creation, "He seals the hand of every man, That all men may know His work." The *Gesenius' Hebrew-Chaldee Lexicon* includes the following with this verse: "i.e. restrains them from labor, hinders them from using their hands."[5] *"How can that be an act of love?"* some might ask. God is not preventing people from work in a bad way. Instead, He is giving man an opportunity to rest. Why is He causing them to stop their work? The end of the verse tells us. It is so man can see God's work. Instead of man laboring to provide for himself and do works in self-effort and self-preservation, God is lovingly giving them a chance to see His divine provision and His work on our behalf. After all, what crops would man have to harvest if God hadn't provided the seed, sun and rain? And, as in Matthew 5:45, this opportunity to rest is for every man. It is not exclusive to only the righteous. God gives everyone the opportunity to allow Him to do the work. God did everything needed for salvation. All man needs to do is receive it. That is the part God cannot do for us. It is our choice; everyone's personal decision and choice.

Clouds

As for the clouds, Job 37:13 NIV discloses, "He brings the clouds to punish people, or to water his earth and show his love." Just like judgement, there can be two sides. This can be seen in the pillar of cloud in the Book of Exodus. To the Israelites, it was a protection and to the Egyptians it was a hindrance.[6] It was an act of God's love.

Stop and Consider

Elihu has his last words at the ready. I can imagine him looking Job straight in the eyes when he tells him to pay close attention to what he is about to say. "Pay attention to this, Job. Stop and consider the wonderful miracles of God!" (Job 37:14 NLT). Stop, Job and really take some time to think about all the marvelous things the Creator of the entire universe has done. Stop, for a moment, looking at your present circumstances. Stop looking to others for approval; stop looking at how you can help yourself. Just stop and look around you. Consider all that God has done in creation. Consider all He has done for you. Consider all He is able to do on your behalf.

Once you have done that, then, look at yourself. Are you able even to come close to what God can do? Is your strength any match to His? How about wisdom; who would come out on top? This is the next line of thought Elihu utilizes. God's ways and thoughts are so much higher than that of any person ever known.

With those closing thoughts and without any delay, Elihu then announces the coming of the Almighty.

> ²²He comes from the north *as* golden *splendor*; With God *is* awesome majesty. ²³*As for* the Almighty, we cannot find Him; *He is* excellent in power, *In* judgment and abundant justice; He does not oppress. (Job 37:22-23 NKJV)

God is so far above us in being mighty, powerful, holy, just, righteous, faithful and loving. I love how he adds that God does not oppress. Stop and consider this Job. Stop and consider all readers of the Book of Job. God is the Almighty. He is so worthy of our praise. He is Love and is not the cause of oppression.

Because of all of this, "Therefore men fear him; he does not regard any who are wise in their own conceit" (Job 37:24 RSV).

---

1 "H7482 - raʿam - Strong's Hebrew Lexicon (nkjv)." Blue Letter Bible. Accessed 25 Oct, 2021.
https://www.blueletterbible.org/lexicon/h7482/nkjv/wlc/0-1/
2 "H6963 - qôl - Strong's Hebrew Lexicon (nkjv)." Blue Letter Bible. Accessed 25 Oct, 2021.
https://www.blueletterbible.org/lexicon/h6963/nkjv/wlc/0-1/
3 See Ex. 9:29
4 "H216 - 'ôr - Strong's Hebrew Lexicon (nkjv)." Blue Letter Bible. Accessed 25 Oct, 2021.
https://www.blueletterbible.org/lexicon/h216/nkjv/wlc/0-1/
5 "H2856 - ḥātam – Gesenius' Hebrew-Chaldee Lexicon (nkjv)." Blue Letter Bible. Accessed 25 Oct, 2021.
https://www.blueletterbible.org/lexicon/h2856/nkjv/wlc/0-1/
6 See Ex. 14:19, 20

Chapter Thirty-Three

JOB CHAPTER 38

RIGHT IN THE MIDST

Oh, how thrilling it is to get to chapter 38! This is when we hear directly from the LORD! It says in verse one that the LORD answered Job out of the storm or whirlwind. The first questions that seem to come to mind are:

1. Why did it take so long for the LORD to answer Job and,

2. Why did the LORD speak from a storm/whirlwind?

Job Chapter 38

In answer to the first question, it helps to answer the second. Looking at First Kings 19, we find the LORD passing by Elijah. Elijah discerned that God was not found in the wind, earthquake or fire. Instead, the LORD was found in the still, small voice. Could it be that the LORD had been speaking to Job all along but Job was not listening to the still, small voice? Or, that Job's complaints and the voices of his comforters were so loud that he was unable to hear the voice of the LORD? Could it be that God turned up the volume so-to-speak? It is possible. However, Job does seem to be quietly listening to Elihu so perhaps the volume wasn't the issue.

Could it be that because Job was in the midst of a storm, God was right there with him? It is not unusual for the LORD to show Himself in ways that reflect the current state of His people. For example, when God spoke to Moses through the burning bush, [1] it reflected how the Israelites had been "burning" in slavery but had not been consumed. Even when the Israelites wandered throughout the wilderness and lived in tents, the LORD lived in their midst in a tent (tabernacle).[2] It is possible that since Job was in a storm, it reveals that God was right there with him.

"Who *is* this who darkens counsel By words without knowledge?" (Job 38:2 NKJV). I think everyone knows the answer but let's unwrap the question. Within the definition of "darkens," is found, "'who is this, who darkens (my) counsel with unwise words;' i.e. strives to hinder it." [3] Likewise, for "knowledge," the same lexicon says, "intelligence, understanding, wisdom."[4] God is clearly asking who is striving to hinder God's counsel by using words void of intelligence, understanding and wisdom. Here is the most credible support for the stance that the words of Job in large part during this portion of his life were the words of a depressed man and not all to be counted as truth. Just because Job said those words and those words were accurately recorded, does not make the statements true. They lacked intelligence, understanding and wisdom and they strived to hinder God's council.

GIRD UP YOUR LOINS

The LORD continues, "Gird up your loins like a man, I will question you, and you shall declare to me" (Job 38:3 RSV). Where else in scripture do we see the notion of girding up ones loins? Ephesians 6:14a NKJV directs the believer to, "Stand therefore, having girded your waist with truth." Could it be that the LORD is saying to Job, *"Get up; dust yourself off! Prepare yourself for a good dose of truth!"* Could it be that Job's spiritual armor wasn't fastened to himself properly? That is one way to make you vulnerable in battle!

COMPARING RÉSUMÉS

Now it is the LORD's chance to be heard. He questions Job and, with the questions, reveals quite a lot. God reveals some of the different facets of His character and His nature. He also reinforces how His ways and thoughts are so far superior to those of a man. It is almost like a comparison of résumés is unlocked. One is able to see a larger question emerge: "Who is more qualified to save Job?" The questions posed by the LORD confirm that God is the Great I AM.[5] God is more capable, more powerful, more knowledgeable, more omnipresent, more creative, more just, more caring, more eternal, wiser and stronger than anyone or anything that can be compared. God's résumé outshines any other. In fact, God is so far above we cannot even articulate the difference.

Hidden within the purpose of the LORD's line of questioning, one can see His love. God is saying to

Job, *"I am fully qualified to save you, help you, provide for you. Please stop trying to do it all yourself. 'Come to Me, all you who labor and are heavy laden, and I will give you rest'.*[6] *I have already made provision for all you need. Just let Me."* Job needed his eyes opened to this and God, in His love, made sure to give Him an eye-opening opportunity.

Q & A

The first set of questions found in Job 38:4-7 involve creation. They highlight God's eternal existence, His creative power, His supreme knowledge, wisdom and understanding. Not only was God there at the time of creation; He was the inventor and engineer of all created. To the smallest detail, God was involved and invested.

The next set of questions in Job 38:8-11 surround the sea. The power of God is evident as He sets boundaries for its waves. Job 38:11 is one of my favorite scriptures on which to stand for healing and the change of circumstances. We are made in God's image[7] and God's Word will not go back to Him without being fulfilled.[8] Therefore, if God can set to the sea boundaries and declare it can go no farther, I believe we, in Jesus' Name, can do the same. In the same way God spoke to the sea saying, "This far you may come, but no farther, And here your proud waves must stop,"[9] if symptoms come upon you, you can tell the sickness in Jesus' Name that it has come this far but this is where it too must stop. The same scripture can be stood upon in any situation or circumstance. *"You've come this far but you can't go any farther…this is where you must stop in Jesus' Name!"*

In Job 38:12-20, God highlights His omnipotence, omnipresence and authority. There is no place that is hidden from God and nothing too difficult for Him.

No Contest

The sarcasm seen in Job 38:21 always causes a smile to come to my face. When the LORD says to Job, "Surely you know, for you were already born! You lived so many years!" (Job 38:21 NIV). Even if Job had been 1000 years old, how would that compare to an eternal God?

So, how is the résumé comparison going? How does Job measure up? I can speak with experience at how difficult it is at times to juggle even the relatively small amount I have on my plate or my to-do list. I acknowledge the grace from God that I require to do what I am called to do daily. Yet God not only does all that is necessary to keep the universe and beyond running, He also takes care of the details which are "not necessary" such as watering a desolate wasteland.[10] Not only that, but God always has the time to watch over and help us in whatever way we will allow. In doing this, God doesn't stress or get tired and He is not stretched for resources. God isn't even restricted by time as God is eternal and outside of time.

---

1 See Ex. 3:2
2 See Ex. 40:34
3 "H2821 - ḥāšak̠ - Gesenius' Hebrew-Chaldee Lexicon (nkjv)." Blue Letter Bible. Accessed 25 Oct, 2021.
https://www.blueletterbible.org/lexicon/h2821/nkjv/wlc/0-1/
4 "H1847 - daʿat̠ - Gesenius' Hebrew-Chaldee Lexicon (nkjv)." Blue Letter Bible. Accessed 25 Oct, 2021.
https://www.blueletterbible.org/lexicon/h1847/nkjv/wlc/0-1/
5 See Ex. 3:14
6 Matt. 11:28 NKJV
7 See Gen. 1:27
8 See Is. 55:11
9 Job 38:11 NKJV
10 Job 38:27

Chapter Thirty-Four

JOB CHAPTER 39

GOD CARES

Chapter 39 solidifies all that is found in chapter 38. The LORD continues to question Job and asks him if he is remotely capable of doing what God does. How often do we think that we can "do it all"? How often do we put it on ourselves to provide for ourselves and to have all the answers? It is so needless. God cares about us and wants to help us and be involved in our lives.

Similarly, it is like the circumstance in the beginning verses of chapter 39.

> ¹Do you know the time when the wild mountain goats bear young? *Or* can you

> mark when the deer gives birth? ²Can you number the months *that* they fulfill? Or do you know the time when they bear young? ³They bow down, They bring forth their young, They deliver their offspring. (Job 39:1-3 NKJV)

God created the mountain goats. He could leave it at that knowing they will go about their days on the earth doing mountain goat-type things. However, God cares enough even about the mountain goats to know when they give birth. And, again, it doesn't tax God to display this level of care for every creature continuously.

STRENGTHS

There are so many things that only God can do. As seen in Job 39:5-12, only God can give freedom to a wild animal. Only God gave certain qualities, attributes and characteristics to animals and mankind. There isn't an animal or person who has their strengths in every area. In the remainder of Job 39, God displays some of the qualities He gave to the ostrich, horse, hawk and eagle. Some had strengths in areas in which others lacked. As the Body of Christ, we know that God has equipped each member to do their part so as, when all members work together, the entire Body is lacking in no area.[1]

---

1 See 1 Cor. 12:14-27

Chapter Thirty-Five

JOB CHAPTER 40

The LORD then, at the start of chapter 40, poses another profound question to Job. "Shall a faultfinder contend with the Almighty? He who argues with God, let him answer it" (Job 40:2 RSV). Along with meaning, "to strive, to make complaint and to quarrel," the Hebrew word used for "contend" in verse 2, can also denote, "to conduct a case or suit (legal), sue."[1] Here is yet another hint at the heavenly court case that has been playing out throughout the Book of Job. Let us not skip over the descriptive word God uses for Job though; the name and label of "faultfinder." This is the only time in the Old Testament this word is used; it can also be translated as "one who reproves."[2] "Reprove" is defined as "to blame, to charge with fault face to face, to chide, to convince of a fault, to disprove."[3] This is what God reveals; Job has been blaming God and charging the Most High with fault. In His question, God presses Job; *"Is the one who brings a court case against Me going to charge Me with fault and blame Me face to face?"*[4] Then God, at the end of verse two, gives Job, who stands to argue the case,[5] the opportunity to answer, testify and respond as a witness.[6]

A CHANGE OF PERSPECTIVE

After all that Job has said throughout the book bearing his name, what is Job's response? It is found in Job 40:4, 5 NKJV, "Behold, I am vile; What shall I answer You? I lay my hand over my mouth. Once I have spoken, but I will not answer; Yes, twice, but I will proceed no further." So after all of Job's ranting throughout multiple chapters; after all of his demands to be able to bring his case before God, now Job is silent? Now Job sees himself as "vile"? What has changed? I believe Job's perspective has changed. He is no longer looking at himself through the eyes of pride. He is no longer seeing his self-righteousness as outshining God's righteousness. That which God showed Job in chapters 38 and 39 opened Job's eyes to how deficient Job is when it comes to comparing himself with God. Job is to the point where he is now showing humility before God. Job no longer claims to have all of the answers. This is where Job's "proud waves stop."[7]

TRUTH

Again, God responds by telling Job to prepare himself for Truth by girding his loins like a man. Then, in Job 40:8 RSV come two more profound questions from the Almighty, "Will you even put me in the wrong? Will you condemn me that you may be justified?" This is the truth revealed about what Job has been doing. Job has been blaming God and making Him out to be unjust all the while promoting his own self-righteousness through works. He has repeatedly said how he is free from guilt and how, consequently, the "guilty verdict" he saw as coming from God was unjustified (thereby accusing God of being unjust).

One can look down on Job for this but there are so many people doing the exact same thing in our present age. How many people shake their fists at God asking, "What did I do to deserve this?" It is all too common for people to self-proclaim themselves guiltless and yet attribute awful characteristics to an all-holy God. I have boldly proclaimed that it is God's desire for all to be healed through the precious stripes of Jesus. It is not unusual for me to be met with resistance from people who are quick to question me. They will say, "Well so and so has prayed and are still sick. Why didn't God heal them?" Often unwittingly, they are saying that the person has done everything right but God has not kept His promise; essentially saying the person is just but God is unjust. There are many reasons why a person, even a just person has not received healing but one thing is certain – it is not due to a fault on God's part. God supplied healing for all at the same time as doing what was necessary to attain salvation for all. Not everyone has received salvation but it is not because of any injustice on God's part.

I cannot begin to explain why certain tragic things happen in specific individual's lives. I am willing, however, to give God the benefit of the doubt and believe the best of Him. When we meet face to face, if He says to me, "Why did you believe so highly of Me? You were wrong to think that way," then I will figure out how to process such information. I am confident, though, that scenario will never happen. As for now, I choose to believe that there must be another explanation for what was at the root of the tragedy. Whether it stemmed from an attack from Satan, reaping a harvest of seed sown (this could be from many generations past) or being rebellious against what God has directed. It could have even stemmed from one of these in the life of another person. I would not attempt to stand in judgement of the why. I am not equipped with all of the information to even make a fully informed guess. God does have the answers, however. He is the One to draw close to for comfort and for answers.

Payback

In digging deeper into verse 8, an interesting insight came into view. The first mention of the Hebrew word "condemn"[8] is found in Exodus 22:9. It speaks of what is to happen in the case where something is stolen. In such a situation where one is accused of stealing, the two parties are to come before God. Whomever God condemns as guilty, was to pay back double what had been stolen. This is interesting because, in the case of Job, Job had accused God of stealing all that was lost including his family, health and prosperity. God knew the behind the scenes of it all though. God knew who the real thief was; the one who came to steal, kill and destroy. It is by God's grace that, in the end, double will be restored back to Job. We will find out more about that in chapter 42.

Requirements

Now, in verses 9-13, God lays out the requirements Job must meet if he is going to be recognized as being able to save himself. All this time Job has been implying that, due to his blamelessness and strict adherence to the law, he can be seen as righteous (a.k.a. not needing a Savior to save him). Let's see if Job can meet the challenge:

Job Chapter 40

> ⁹Have you an arm like God? Or can you thunder with a voice like His? ¹⁰Then adorn yourself *with* majesty and splendor, And array yourself with glory and beauty. ¹¹Disperse the rage of your wrath; Look on everyone *who is* proud, and humble him. ¹²Look on everyone *who is* proud, *and* bring him low; Tread down the wicked in their place. ¹³Hide them in the dust together, Bind their faces in hidden *darkness*. (Job 40:9-13 NKJV)

According to verse 14, it is only if Job is able to fulfil all of these prerequisites that God will acknowledge that Job can save himself. God shines the light so brightly on Job to reveal that it is impossible for him to save himself. Job, like all of mankind, needs a Savior. In God's love and mercy, He reveals the Grace message to Job.

In fact, God's love is evident through His entire interaction with Job. If one looks through the lens of love, they can see God's love in wanting to speak with Job, in His wanting to set the record straight so Job can know God's true heart toward him and in God's desire to reveal Himself and bring understanding, wisdom and revelation. It shows God's longing to have a close relationship with His creation.

BEHEMOTH

In verse 15 to the close of chapter 40, God describes a creature called, "Behemoth." No doubt there are many thoughts and opinions about what kind of animal such an illustration describes. Whether it is a large animal today or a dinosaur-like creature from old is not necessarily required to solve the mystery in order to gain understanding in this passage.

It sounds as though the behemoth represented the largest, strongest, mightiest animal in God's creation. It can be hidden as well as in plain sight. It is unfazed by anything and everything. It is undaunted by anything and yet it will bow before God and submit to Him.

The behemoth can be a picture of any situation that looks supremely powerful and unbeatable; those instances we face which seem insurmountable. We in ourselves may be no match for such a giant but, as Luke 1:37 NKJV says, "For with God nothing will be impossible." With God, behemoths must bow.

God revealed to Job another aspect of His all-powerful omnipotence. At the same time it shows both Job's inadequacies and His willingness to stand with Job in those seemingly impossible situations to ensure victory. God is willing to help Job in the situation he currently faces if Job will stop trying to save himself and allow God to work on his behalf.

---

1 "H7378 - rîb - Strong's Hebrew Lexicon (nkjv)." Blue Letter Bible. Accessed 27 Oct, 2021.
https://www.blueletterbible.org/lexicon/h7378/nkjv/wlc/0-1/
2 "H3250 - yissôr - Strong's Hebrew Lexicon (nkjv)." Blue Letter Bible. Accessed 27 Oct, 2021.
https://www.blueletterbible.org/lexicon/h3250/nkjv/wlc/0-1/
3 Webster, Noah. "Reprove." Webster's Dictionary 1828, 27 Oct. 2021, http://www.webstersdictionary1828.com/Dictionary/reprove. Accessed 27 Oct. 2021.
4 Author's interpretation
5 "H3198 - yāḵaḥ - Strong's Hebrew Lexicon (nkjv)." Blue Letter Bible. Accessed 27 Oct, 2021.
https://www.blueletterbible.org/lexicon/h3198/nkjv/wlc/0-1/
6 "H6030 - ʿānâ - Strong's Hebrew Lexicon (nkjv)." Blue Letter Bible. Accessed 27 Oct, 2021.
https://www.blueletterbible.org/lexicon/h6030/nkjv/wlc/0-1/
7 See Job 38:11
8 "H7561 - rāšaʿ - Strong's Hebrew Lexicon (nkjv)." Blue Letter Bible. Accessed 27 Oct, 2021.
https://www.blueletterbible.org/lexicon/h7561/nkjv/wlc/0-1/

Chapter Thirty-Six

JOB CHAPTER 41

LEVIATHAN

Similar to the behemoth in chapter 40, God describes another creature in chapter 41. Again, in this case, it is not necessary to debate the identity of this creature; it is more imperative to see the message. Compared to the behemoth, the leviathan seems much more menacing. It appears to be representative of one's biggest threat or adversary. Job 41:9a NKJV asserts, "Indeed, any hope of overcoming him is false" and verse 26 makes it clear that no weapon formed by human hands are any match for leviathan. Even though leviathan seems to be quite indomitable, it is no match for God Almighty. He alone is the One able to conquer this foe. God is full and complete in

His omnipotence. However, in His love and grace, God made covenant with mankind. Romans 8:31b NKJV confirms, "If God *is* for us, who *can be* against us?" With God on our side, there is no foe, threat or adversary that cannot be conquered. This is how "we are more than conquerors through Him who loved us."[1] As imposing a circumstance or threat may be, we need not fear with God on our side. Grasping the true revelation of this fact is how "perfect love casts out fear."[2] If we have no need of fearing the ultimate threat, then we really have nothing to fear. It is solely because of God's great love that we need not fear.

> As imposing a circumstance or threat may be, we need not fear with God on our side.

God brings up an additional point in Job 41:10, 11 NKJV, "No one *is so* fierce that he would dare stir him up. Who then is able to stand against Me? Who has preceded Me, that I should pay *him?* Everything under heaven is Mine." With regard to Job, he has proven his inability to conquer this adversary and yet has stood in judgement of God. He called for a battle of sorts with God. He has wanted to debate and accuse God of lack of justice. If Job is unable to bring defeat to something only God can vanquish, then what chance does Job stand against the Omnipotent God?

Continuing on, God also points out that He owes nothing to anyone. God chooses to love us, chooses to help us, and chooses to save us. It is not something He was ever obligated to do. He does everything for us because of His great love for us.

---

1 Rom. 8:37 NKJV
2 1 John 4:18 NKJV

Chapter Thirty-Seven

JOB CHAPTER 42

REVEALED

Well, we made it! Chapter 42 is here at last. We have journeyed through the Book of Job and discovered quite a lot. We have seen a court case unfold before us. Let's see where Job is at now.

"I know that you can do all things; no purpose of yours can be thwarted" (Job 42:2 NIV). If one breaks down the Hebrew meanings of the words used in verse two, some insights come into focus. The following shows possible translations:

I know = *yāda‘* = to know by experience[1]
that you can do = *yākōl* = have power[2]

all things = *kōl* = the whole³
no purpose of yours = *mᵊzimmâ* = counsel⁴
can be thwarted = *bāṣar* = make inaccessible⁵

It could be that Job was saying, *"I know intimately Your complete powers and abilities and none of Your counsel will be made inaccessible."* Now we are able to see what Job has learned. After the revelation God gave Job, he now has a more intimate knowledge of who God is and the power He has. It appears that Job also sees that God is not hiding from nor ignoring him. None of God's counsel will be made inaccessible. Jeremiah 33:3 NKJV says it well, "Call to Me, and I will answer you, and show you great and mighty things, which you do not know."

Verse 3 reveals that Job heard what God had asked him in Job 38:2. However, there are some differences in what God said and Job's "quote." In Job 38:2 NKJV, God said, "Who *is* this who darkens counsel By words without knowledge?" The word "darkens" originates in the Hebrew word *ḥāšak* and is described as "to be dark (as withholding light)."⁶ In contrast, Job 42:3 NKJV says, "Who *is* this who hides counsel without knowledge?" Instead of repeating the word *ḥāšak*, Job uses *ʿālam*, which is described as "to veil from sight."⁷ It is as though God was asking Job why he tried to make God's counsel appear to be dark and without the light of truth. Job seems to admit to hiding God's counsel; perhaps hiding the truth. By Job trying to conceal the benefits of God's counsel, he tried to make himself look better. Job also omits the "words without knowledge part." Even so, Job admits as he continues that he indeed, "uttered what [he] did not understand, Things too wonderful for [him], which [he] did not know" Job 42:3b NKJV. Again, this confirms once more how to perceive much of what Job said throughout the Book of Job. He was largely speaking out of ignorance.

Eye Opening Experience

Thankfully, much has changed! Job declares in Job 42:5 NKJV, "I have heard of You by the hearing of the ear, But now my eye sees You." Oh how wonderful. One can see what had occurred. It is something to which many of us can relate. Thinking we know everything there is to know about someone or something simply through hearsay, rumor or head knowledge. What beliefs did Job hold concerning God simply because of what experience or tradition or others said? When God blessed Job with what is found in chapters 38-41, Job was able to see God for himself. Of course, this is not just seeing God physically; it is a deeper revelation of who He is. This is what God desires for each of us. In His love, God yearns for us to know Him intimately. If we do, we can no longer be duped and deceived into believing lies about Him. Also, we will know His heart which in turn will, as stated multiple times before, allow us to live fearlessly for His perfect love casts out such fear.[8]

Revelation

What was the great revelation that Job saw? Was it God's power, God's faithfulness, God's love? It could be all of the above. Could it have been a revelation of God's ability and desire to save? Could it have been that Job saw the fullness of the Grace message? Job had been attempting to save himself. His hope was that, if he was good enough, holy enough, blameless enough, it would be enough to save him. He learned that he could never be good enough on his own. He could never do enough to erase the death sentence brought about by the fall of mankind. Job learned that he needed a Savior; a Mediator who could accomplish for him what he could not. He learned that God, in

His love, mercy and grace had a plan of salvation for mankind. All Job needed to do was receive it and allow God to do the saving.

What was the result of this revelation? It can be found in Job 42:6 NIV, "Therefore I despise myself and repent in dust and ashes." Going back to the original Hebrew,[9] I can see this as a possible rendering as well: *"Therefore, on account of this, I reject what I said out of ignorance and out of what I said based on rumor and I repent (have a change of thinking) and grieve*[10] *what I said before. I will now think and say what I know for myself to be true about God from my own personal experience and relationship with Him."*[11] The New American Standard Bible says that Job retracted what he had said. He learned it wasn't accurate and took it all back.

> In His love, God yearns for us to know Him intimately. If we do, we can no longer be duped and deceived into believing lies about Him.

Job repented in the truest sense of the word. "Repent" is not equal to an apology. It is a turning of direction and a changing of one's mind.[12] Job had a major shift in his thinking and his thoughts toward God.

A Clean Slate

At the moment when Job repented, the matter was settled with God. God saw that Job was now speaking the truth about Him. "And so it was, after the LORD had spoken these words to Job, that the LORD said to Eliphaz the Temanite, 'My wrath is aroused against you and your two friends, for you have not spoken of Me *what is* right, as My servant Job *has*" (Job 42:7 NKJV). The Hebrew for "right" gives a sense of the stability of something that has been firmly established.[13] All of the words without knowledge that Job had spoken was wiped clean from all heavenly accounts the minute Job repented. All God saw was the right words Job spoke. It shows God's faithfulness in forgiveness found in First John 1:9 and Hebrews 8:12. Likewise, the clean slate given to Job through God's forgiveness is seen in the Book of James. In James 5:11, God speaks of Job's perseverance; He does not bring up Job's idle words or misguided steps. It, at the same time, highlights the love of God in His compassion and mercy. You can see the joy of the Father speaking about how Job persevered so many years before. We can see how Job went from being someone who was once mixed up to someone seen as an example of an overcomer.

> [11]Indeed we count them blessed who endure. You have heard of the perseverance of Job and seen the end intended by the Lord - that the Lord is very compassionate and merciful. (James 5:11 NKJV)

The three companions Eliphaz, Bildad and Zophar still had something left undone. It was made clear that what they had said was not correct either. God calls what the three had done "folly." God did not leave the three in that condition though. He, in His love and mercy, gave the three an opportunity to make things right.

> Now therefore, take for yourselves seven bulls and seven rams, go to My servant Job, and offer up for yourselves a burnt offering; and My servant Job shall pray for you. For I will accept him, lest I deal with you *according to your* folly; because

you have not spoken of Me *what is* right, as My servant Job *has*. (Job 42:8 NKJV)

It is interesting to note Elihu was not included in this list. Therefore, we can conclude Elihu's words were right before God.

About the Sacrifice

Job 42:8a laid out the directions for the sacrifice. They were to bring seven bulls and seven rams to Job so he could offer them as a burnt offering. The number seven represents perfection or completeness.[14] In presenting seven of each animal, it would represent a perfect and complete offering; one in which nothing is left out or overlooked. This sacrifice would not leave anything undone or incomplete. The word translated as "bullock" comes from the Hebrew word *par*.[15] It is first used in association with a sacrifice in Exodus 24:5. In this case, it was for a fellowship or peace offering to the LORD. It was also used as part of a blood covenant between the LORD and the Israelites with Moses. Likewise, the first mention of a ram being offered was part of the blood covenant between the LORD and Abram in Genesis 15.

In this case, the three were to present their offerings as a burnt offering. Leviticus 1:4 NKJV asserts that during a burnt offering, "he shall put his hand on the head of the burnt offering, and it will be accepted on his behalf to make atonement for him." These offerings would be "a sweet aroma to the LORD" (Lev.1:9b NKJV).

Job was, once more, back in the position of high priest. He was able to present their sacrifices before God. Job was able to pray with his prayers being powerful and effective.[16] God promised He would accept Job's prayer. This being said, it was still a free choice for the three. They could have continued on their way without any form of repentance. Thankfully, they did do precisely as God had directed and God accepted Job's prayer.

RESTORATION

Job, through this repentance and in his obedience in praying for his friends, got back under the Shadow of the Almighty; he got back into the protection of the hedge God had for him. This enabled the LORD to make Job prosperous once again. Job 42:10 NKJV confirms, "And the LORD restored Job's losses when he prayed for his friends. Indeed the LORD gave Job twice as much as he had before."

THE VISITORS

God begins to restore everything back to Job and what happens? "Then all his brothers, all his sisters, and all those who had been his acquaintances before, came to him and ate food with him in his house" (Job 42:11a NKJV). Had any of these people visited Job when he was in the midst of the bad times? Had everyone avoided Job? If so, what was their reasoning? Were they afraid Job was contagious? Did they feel unqualified to help Job? Did they stay away because they couldn't stand to see Job in such pain and agony? Did they feel Job no longer had anything to offer them? Did Job refuse their company? The answer to this can only come, no doubt, through divine revelation. What we do know is that they did return and Job welcomed them graciously.

What was the purpose of these visitors? It says in the remainder of Job 42:11b RSV that, "they showed him sympathy and comforted him for all the evil that the LORD had brought upon him; and each of them gave him a piece of money and a ring of gold." The word for sympathy[17] and comfort[18] in verse 11 are the same words used in Job 2:11 when it speaks of what the three friends had come to do. They appear to be in the same cycle of folly that had once encompassed Eliphaz, Bildad and Zophar. This is clear when it confirms they were focusing on "all the evil that the LORD had brought upon him" Job 42:11 RSV. They were just as blind to the fact that the evil was not from God. Could they not see the restoration God was doing in Job's life? Were they too busy looking back at the time of trouble to see the renewal? At any rate, these visitors played a part in the restoration whether they could see it or not. Each of them brought to Job money and gold. Additionally, these people giving back to Job could stem from something we discussed previously about a thief, once caught, being required to pay back double in Exodus 22:9.

Seeing Double

> Now the LORD blessed the latter days of Job more than his beginning: for he had fourteen thousand sheep, six thousand camels, one thousand yoke of oxen, and one thousand female donkeys. (Job 42:12 NKJV)

Seen here is an exact doubling of the livestock Job had in Job 1:3. The number of sons and daughters in Job 42:13, however, matches exactly to those mentioned in Job 1:2. In each case, Job is shown to have seven sons and three daughters. Why would these numbers not have doubled? It is because Job never lost his first ten children. Even though they had died, Job would see them again. His children would have been in Paradise. Reading between the lines a little, too, the fact that Job has more children implies that Job's wife was also still in the picture.

"In all the land were found no women *so* beautiful as the daughters of Job; and their father gave them an inheritance among their brothers" (Job 42:15 NKJV).

It shows the abundance in which Job was living to see that he gave his daughters an inheritance along with his sons. No doubt Job also gave them the gift of wisdom and understanding he gained through his newly established intimacy with God. The revelation of God's unconditional love toward all of us undoubtedly played into Job's decision to lavish his children each with an inheritance.

"After this Job lived one hundred and forty years, and saw his children and grandchildren for four generations" (Job 42:16 NKJV). This difficult time Job experienced was such a tiny portion of his life. It is like Romans 8:18 NKJV, "For I consider that the sufferings of this present time are not worthy to be compared with the glory which shall be revealed in us." No matter what we might go through during our lives on earth, we know that, with Jesus as our Savior, we will have ahead days of glory.

> He loves us so much that He made a way for all of us to be restored back to Him. While it cost Him immensely, it comes to each of us freely. It is not difficult. It is received by faith.

"So Job died, old and full of days" (Job 42:17 NKJV). The Hebrew word for "full" means "satisfied." [19] Just like in Psalm 91, Job experienced the promise of, "With long life I will satisfy him, And show him My salvation" (Psalm 91:16 NKJV).

This is where the Book of Job ends. However, it does not seem a coincidence that the next chapter in the Bible is Psalm 1. Psalm 1 seems to sum up some of the lessons found in the Book of Job.

It is my hope the journey we have taken through the Book of Job while looking through the lens of love has given a greater revelation of God's love. He loves us so much that He made a way for all of us to be restored back to Him. While it cost Him immensely, it comes to each of us freely. It is not difficult. It is received by faith. Consequently, what do we see when we look through the lens of love? Grace. God loves us so much that He gave us grace so we could be with Him and be in His fullness forever.

---

1 "H3045 - yāḏaʿ - Strong's Hebrew Lexicon (nkjv)." Blue Letter Bible. Accessed 27 Oct, 2021.
https://www.blueletterbible.org/lexicon/h3045/nkjv/wlc/0-1/
2 "H3201 - yāḵōl - Strong's Hebrew Lexicon (nkjv)." Blue Letter Bible. Accessed 27 Oct, 2021.
https://www.blueletterbible.org/lexicon/h3201/nkjv/wlc/0-1/
3 "H3605 - kōl - Strong's Hebrew Lexicon (nkjv)." Blue Letter Bible. Accessed 27 Oct, 2021.
https://www.blueletterbible.org/lexicon/h3605/nkjv/wlc/0-1/
4 "H4209 - mᵉzimmâ – Gesenius' Hebrew-Chaldee Lexicon (nkjv)." Blue Letter Bible. Accessed 27 Oct, 2021.
https://www.blueletterbible.org/lexicon/h4209/nkjv/wlc/0-1/
5 "H1219 - bāṣar - Strong's Hebrew Lexicon (nkjv)." Blue Letter Bible. Accessed 27 Oct, 2021.
https://www.blueletterbible.org/lexicon/h1219/nkjv/wlc/0-1/
6 "H2821 - ḥāšaḵ - Strong's Hebrew Lexicon (nkjv)." Blue Letter Bible. Accessed 27 Oct, 2021.
https://www.blueletterbible.org/lexicon/h2821/nkjv/wlc/0-1/
7 "H5956 - ʿālam - Strong's Hebrew Lexicon (nkjv)." Blue Letter Bible. Accessed 27 Oct, 2021.
https://www.blueletterbible.org/lexicon/h5956/nkjv/wlc/0-1/
8 See 1 John 4:18 NKJV
9 https://biblehub.com/strongs/job/42-6.htm
10 "H5162 - nāḥam – Gesenius' Hebrew-Chaldee Lexicon (nkjv)." Blue Letter Bible. Accessed 27 Oct, 2021.
https://www.blueletterbible.org/lexicon/h5162/nkjv/wlc/0-1/
11 Author's interpretation
12 "Repent." *Merriam-Webster.com Dictionary*, Merriam-Webster, https://www.merriam-webster.com/dictionary/repent. Accessed 27 Oct. 2021.
13 "H3559 - kûn - Strong's Hebrew Lexicon (nkjv)." Blue Letter Bible. Accessed 27 Oct, 2021.
https://www.blueletterbible.org/lexicon/h3559/nkjv/wlc/0-1/
14 Cioccolanti, Steve. The Divine Code – A Prophetic Encyclopedia of Numbers, Vol. 1. Discover Media, p. 114, 2009-2019. Kindle edition.

15 "H6499 - par - Strong's Hebrew Lexicon (nkjv)." Blue Letter Bible. Accessed 27 Oct, 2021.
https://www.blueletterbible.org/lexicon/h6499/nkjv/wlc/0-1/
16 See James 5:16b NIV
17 "H5110 - nûḏ - Strong's Hebrew Lexicon (nkjv)." Blue Letter Bible. Accessed 27 Oct, 2021.
https://www.blueletterbible.org/lexicon/h5110/nkjv/wlc/0-1/
18 "H5162 - nāḥam - Strong's Hebrew Lexicon (nkjv)." Blue Letter Bible. Accessed 27 Oct, 2021.
https://www.blueletterbible.org/lexicon/h5162/nkjv/wlc/0-1/
19 "H7649 - śāḇēaʿ - Strong's Hebrew Lexicon (nkjv)." Blue Letter Bible. Accessed 27 Oct, 2021.
https://www.blueletterbible.org/lexicon/h7649/nkjv/wlc/0-1/

Chapter Thirty-Eight

THE THORN IN THE FLESH

Now that we have thoroughly discussed the Book of Job, let us now turn to investigating the infamous "thorn in the flesh." There have been countless dialogues about what exactly Paul referred when he wrote Second Corinthians 12:7. Many, many, many people have, throughout the years, chosen to believe some of the worst about God simply because of improper teaching on the matter. Let us, therefore, see what we find when we put tradition and doctrine aside and view this part of scripture through the lens of love.

A few arguments and misconceptions arise concerning this topic. Quite often people say that God sent the thorn to Paul in order for Paul to gain humility. They claim that the thorn was a sickness of some sort. They are often convinced that, after Paul prayed multiple times to God to deliver him from the thorn, God denied his request.

In this section of the book, I will attempt to examine the following:

- What is a thorn in the flesh?
- Who sent the thorn?
- Why was the thorn sent?
- What was Paul's response?
- What was God's response?
- What were the results?
- What could this thorn really have been?
- What about humility?

Hopefully, once this is thoroughly examined, it will be clear as to how "God is Love" fits in with this account. For far too long, what Job and Paul went through has been cause for people not to trust God completely. If it is established once and for all that GOD IS LOVE, there is no limit to what God will be able to achieve in and through His people. Before we continue, however, let's take a look at the reference scripture:

> [7]And lest I should be exalted above measure through the abundance of the revelations, there was given to me a thorn in the flesh, the messenger of Satan to buffet me, lest I should be exalted above measure. [8]For this thing I besought the Lord thrice, that it might depart from me. [9]And he said unto me, My grace is sufficient for thee: for my strength is made perfect in weakness. Most gladly therefore will I rather glory

in my infirmities, that the power of Christ may rest upon me. ¹⁰Therefore I take pleasure in infirmities, in reproaches, in necessities, in persecutions, in distresses for Christ's sake: for when I am weak, then am I strong. (2 Cor. 12:7-10 KJV)

WHAT IS THE THORN IN THE FLESH?

Many people through the years have attempted to give name to what Paul's thorn actually was. Sadly, too often, they have supposed it to be a sickness of some kind. Given time and thought, no doubt many things could be attributed to what exactly a thorn in the flesh could be. It is likely wise, however, to allow the Bible to interpret for us. Some insight can be gained by reading Numbers 33:55.

> 'But if you do not drive out the inhabitants of the land from before you, then it shall be that those whom you let remain shall be irritants in your eyes and thorns in your sides, and they shall harass you in the land where you dwell. (Num. 33:55 NKJV)

Here, "thorns" describe an irritant or a nuisance. "Thorns in your sides" is a phrase that could be equated to our modern day idiom "pain in the neck." God was warning the Israelites that if they did not rid the land of its current inhabitants, that they would be an annoyance to them. As one can see in the Old Testament, this was, in fact, true. The people the Israelites allowed to stay in the Promised Land did become irritants and nuisances to the people of God.

Thorns were also symbolic of the curse. Genesis 3:18 is the first mention of "thorns" and it is in direct relation with the curse that came upon the land after Adam's fall.

> [17]Then to Adam He said, "Because you have heeded the voice of your wife, and have eaten from the tree of which I commanded you, saying, 'You shall not eat of it':
> "Cursed *is* the ground for your sake;
> In toil you shall eat *of* it
> All the days of your life.
> [18]Both thorns and thistles it shall bring forth for you,
> And you shall eat the herb of the field.
> [19]In the sweat of your face you shall eat bread
> Till you return to the ground,
> For out of it you were taken;
> For dust you *are,*
> And to dust you shall return."
> (Gen. 3:17-19 NKJV)

We can conclude one piece of the puzzle: the thorn in the flesh was likely some kind of irritant or nuisance to Paul. It is also curse-related.

WHO SENT THE THORN?

Tradition would have us believe that God sent Paul this thorn in the flesh in order to teach him something. However, in Second Corinthians 12:7, it clearly states that the thorn was a "messenger from Satan." As we discussed in the beginning chapters of this book, we know that God is not conspiring with Satan. They do not have a partnership nor do they collaborate for the betterment or demise of humans.

From this, we can find another puzzle piece: the thorn came from Satan, not from God.

WHY WAS THE THORN SENT?

Again, it is often taught that God sent the thorn to Paul to humble him. We can hopefully agree at this point that God did not send the thorn to Paul and did not "allow" the thorn in order to teach Paul something. What does God's Word actually say about humility? Does it say that God will do something to make or keep us humble? There are overwhelming amounts of scriptures that support the idea that we are to actually "humble ourselves." Daniel 10:12, Second Chronicles 7:14, Ezra 8:21 are just a few! Along with this, the Bible supports the idea that those who exalt themselves will be humbled (Matthew 23:12, Luke 14:11). So what exactly is happening in Second Corinthians? Was Paul conceited, full of himself or prideful? Just the opposite! Paul was consistent in pointing people to focus on Jesus…not on himself. In fact, one chapter prior, in Second Corinthians 11, Paul states that he had humbled himself! "Did I commit sin in humbling myself that you might be exalted, because I preached the gospel of God to you free of charge?" (2 Cor. 11:7 NKJV).

What is meant, then, by Paul's writing, "…lest I should be exalted above measure by the abundance of the revelations…" (2 Cor. 12:7a NKJV)? Could it be that Satan did not want to see Paul exalted above measure? The more revelation Paul received from God, the more that revelation was spread throughout the area. People were listening intently to what Paul had to say. To say that Paul had revelation concerning the Gospel of Christ would be an understatement. He knew the Torah backwards and forwards and was easily able to see Jesus depicted there and prove with scripture that Jesus is the Messiah.[1] Armed with this message, Paul went throughout the towns and villages spreading the Word and teaching anyone and everyone who would listen. In Acts 24:5 NKJV, Paul is even accused of spreading his message "among all the Jews throughout the **world**." Needless to say, the kingdom of darkness would not have wanted this to continue. Therefore, the "messenger of Satan" was dispatched to try to hinder Paul's work in any way it could. As such, I believe this refers to the enemy's attempt to thwart the Gospel from going forth.

The next piece to the puzzle: the thorn could have been sent to try to hinder the spread of the Gospel.

WHAT WAS PAUL'S RESPONSE?

We have established that it is more than likely the thorn in the flesh was an attempt by the enemy to thwart the spreading of the Gospel by Paul. What does Paul do? What do most believers do when seemingly under attack? We, most often, will turn to prayer. Paul did as well. He "besought the Lord thrice, that it might depart" (2 Cor. 12:8 KJV). Three times Paul asked God to take the thorn away.

It is important to note here that Paul must have believed that the thorn was not part of God's will for his life. We know this because, otherwise, Paul would not have sought God three times for its removal. Instead, he would have counted it as part of the suffering he knew he would have to endure. Remember, God revealed to Paul what he must suffer for His sake.[2]

WHAT WAS GOD'S RESPONSE?

What exactly was God's response? Many would have you believe that God denied Paul's request. So, what happened to, "The prayer of a righteous person is powerful and effective."[3] In addition, what about, "If you ask anything in My name, I will do it."[4] God rejecting Paul's plea does not line up with a God of love who keeps His Word. The scripture says in the same book of Second Corinthians that, "For all the promises of God in Him are Yes, and in Him Amen, to the glory of God through us" (2 Cor. 1:20 NKJV). It does not say that God says, "NO" in answer to our prayers. Instead, it promises that God will keep His Word.

Instead, God's response was, "My grace is sufficient for thee: for my strength is made perfect in weakness" (2 Cor. 12:9a KJV). God told Paul that His grace was sufficient for him. What does this mean? Does it mean that God would give Paul the grace to endure the thorn? I don't believe so. Instead, I believe God meant something much greater. To see it clearly, let's take a closer look at Paul himself.

A CLOSER LOOK AT PAUL

I believe that, like us, Paul was learning and growing in Christ as time went on. I do not think that he instantly knew everything in one big poof at his conversion on the road to Damascus. He was being taught along the way by Holy Spirit, fellow believers and the Word of God. As various circumstances arose, Paul was trained in how to handle them. He then relayed what he learned through his communications with the Jews, the nations and the Church.

At the point at which Paul was writing to the Corinthians we know a few things about him. We know that he:

- was born again (Acts 9:5)
- was filled with the Holy Spirit with the evidence of speaking in other tongues (Acts 9:17, 1 Cor. 14:18)
- knew the Word of God (Acts 9:22, 15:35, 17:3)
- had the Name of Jesus and the authority to use it (Matt. 28:18, 19; Mark 11:23, 24; John 14:13, 15:16)
- knew the fruit of the Spirit (Gal. 5:22, 23)
- knew the power of Communion (1 Cor. 11:17-33)

- knew the message of salvation through grace (Acts 15:11, Gal. 2:21, Eph. 2:8)
- knew the power of the Cross (1 Cor. 1:18)
- was led by Holy Spirit (Acts 13:4, 16:6, Gal. 5:16-18)
- knew the power of God to heal (Acts 14:10)
- knew about God's miraculous signs and wonders (Gal. 3:5)
- knew we were redeemed from the curse (Gal. 3:13)

We know these about Paul because it was either written about him in the Book of Acts or because Paul taught about them in the epistles he had written up to this point. Having established these points, I believe God's response to Paul was a very powerful one. One that would have sounded something like this: *"Paul, you are a born again, Holy Spirit-filled child of the Most High God. You have the Word of God, the fruit of the Spirit, the ability to speak in tongues, the Name of Jesus and the authority to use it. Therefore, YOU get rid of the thorn. YOU tell it to go in the Name of Jesus! And, where your abilities to get the job done aren't quite sufficient, MY GRACE is sufficient to get you the rest of the way!"* God was showing Paul that grace encompasses so much more than undeserved favor in being saved. God was showing Paul that God's grace could be adapted to any situation!

God recognizes that Paul is still learning and being trained up in matters of faith. It is during this "thorn in the flesh" time that God was taking the training wheels off and getting Paul to move in deeper truths. Paul has authority as a believer in Christ. Three times Paul had asked God to do for Paul what God had already equipped Paul to do within that authority.

If the thorn had have been some sort of sickness, Paul would have already known what to do to get deliverance. He used the Name of Jesus and his authority as a believer to lay hands on the sick multiple times. This thorn was a new situation for Paul. He was learning how to handle it. It could have been that, up until now, in any similar sort of situation, he prayed and God's grace got him the rest of the way. This time, however, it was time for Paul to grow in operation of his position and authority in Christ.

> Paul has authority as a believer in Christ. Three times Paul had asked God to do for Paul what God had already equipped Paul to do within that authority.

God has given believers in Christ such a vast toolbox from which to operate. Along with the list above, we also have the armor of God found in Ephesians 6. So often, believers are waiting on God to do something about a certain situation and wondering why He is not moving. Each time, though, God has provided the way for us to (in Jesus' Name) get the job done. At some point, we all have to take the training wheels off and start using the tools He has supplied so generously and mercifully.

This is why it is so exciting to find Second Corinthians 12:9b-10 KJV. It was when Paul's abilities lacked in some way to get the job done that God's grace would swoop in and finish the job! It was in Paul's weakness that he saw God's grace in action!

> [9b]for my strength is made perfect in weakness. Most gladly therefore will I rather glory in my infirmities, that the

power of Christ may rest upon me. ¹⁰Therefore I take pleasure in infirmities, in reproaches, in necessities, in persecutions, in distresses for Christ's sake: for when I am weak, then am I strong. (2 Cor. 12:9b-10 KJV)

How thrilling!! In this case, God was showing Paul that when God's SUPER hooks up with Paul's NATURAL, it will lead to SUPERNATURAL results. The same is true for each and every believer in Christ! Praise God!!

WHAT WERE THE RESULTS?

What were the results then? Did Paul live forever with the thorn in the flesh? Did he ever do anything about it? Did he just learn to live with it? Identifying what we know about Paul, and knowing that he recognizes believers as being "more than conquerors,"[5] I would find it hard to believe that he did nothing. It will prove helpful to try to reason what the situation could have been given all of the puzzle pieces we have found in this journey together.

Puzzle Pieces:
- the thorn in the flesh was likely some kind of irritant or nuisance to Paul
- the thorn was curse-related
- the thorn came from Satan; not from God
- the thorn could have been sent to try to hinder the spread of the Gospel
- three times Paul asked God to take the thorn away
- Paul was fully equipped by God with the authority of the believer
- God told Paul that His grace is sufficient for Paul

WHAT COULD THIS THORN REALLY HAVE BEEN?

Looking through the scriptures, are there any instances in which the above puzzle pieces fit? I believe there is. If one looks in Acts 16:16-18, one can find a situation in which Paul was irritated for many days due to a girl who was following them.

> [16] "Now it happened, as we went to prayer, that a certain slave girl possessed with a spirit of divination met us, who brought her masters much profit by fortune-telling. [17]This girl followed Paul and us, and cried out, saying, 'These men are the servants of the Most High God, who proclaim to us the way of salvation.' [18]And this she did for many days. But Paul, greatly annoyed, turned and said to the spirit, 'I command you in the name of Jesus Christ to come out of her.' And he came out that very hour." (Acts 16:16-18 NKJV)

A clear portrait is revealed when each of the puzzle pieces is neatly fit together:

- The wicked spirit operating in and through this young girl was "**a messenger of Satan.**"
- She, with her constant declarations, proved to "**buffet**" Paul in an attempt to **hinder the spreading of the Gospel**. *"How?"* one may ask, *"She was speaking truth; the men were God's servants proclaiming the way of salvation!"* Yes, it is true what she said but it was also distracting people from the message Paul was preaching. It was drawing attention away

The Thorn in the Flesh

from the Gospel and putting it on both Paul and the girl's "talents." (Let me be clear that the girl was not talented at all…a familiar spirit was feeding her information in order to deceive the listeners.)

- This went on for **many days**. Could it have been enough time for Paul to seek God three times for the annoyance to be removed? I think it is more than plausible.
- Paul was "**greatly annoyed.**"
- And, finally, **Paul spoke in the Name of Jesus** and the **demon came out of her** that very hour.

ANOTHER POSSIBILITY

If this explanation does not satisfy, I have heard another thought on the subject. Robin D. Bullock, author of *God is Absolutely Good*, suggests that the "thorn" was part of Paul's past. Since Paul had spent so much of his "pre-conversion" life persecuting Christians, a "**messenger of Satan**" could have stood accusing Paul repeatedly that he was not worthy of preaching the Gospel. "**Buffeting**" him into a life of condemnation and setting him up to give up preaching because of his past. Obviously, Paul would have risen up with the knowledge that he is now a new creation in Christ Jesus[6] and there is no longer any condemnation for those who are believers.[7] In this, Paul would have still become an overcomer.

Either way, Paul did not live long with this thorn. And, any personal limitations Paul had would have just shone the light on God's glorious grace.

WHAT ABOUT HUMILITY?

There is a doctrine which has led people to believe that Paul needed humbling. As stated previously, it is scriptural for believers to humble themselves. Looking through the Book of Acts and the epistles written up until and including Second Corinthians, I endeavored to see if Paul really was full of himself and deficient of humility. I was unable to find any circumstance or scripture to back up the claim. Instead, I found instance after instance where Paul would point people to Jesus. Paul had the pedigree to "deserve" man's praise and accolades. In Philippians 3:5-6, Paul lists his "credentials." He goes on to say in the verses that follow that he does not give any glory to these but looks only to Jesus.

Paul shows his humility in being led by Holy Spirit to know what to say and where to say it. He went only to the places to which Holy Spirit led. Also, Acts 14 shows that, while in Lystra, the crowd was treating Paul as if he was a Greek god. If Paul was in it for the "royal treatment," he would not have stopped them from showering him with praise. Instead, it was revolting to Paul and he strove to put an end to the nonsense.

Furthermore, Paul states in Galatians 1:10 NKJV, "For do I now persuade men, or God? Or do I seek to please men? For if I still pleased men, I would not be a bondservant of Christ." Paul is clearly not seeking man's approval nor looking to bolster his own ego.

---

1 See Acts 18:28
2 See Acts 9:16
3 James 5:16 NIV
4 John 14:14 NKJV
5 See Rom. 8:37
6 See 2 Cor. 5:17
7 See Rom. 8:1

Chapter Thirty-Nine

COMPARISONS BETWEEN JOB AND PAUL

Throughout this study, some comparisons have emerged between Job, Paul and their written accounts. Exploring them will prove fruitful in our mission to see where Love stands amongst them.

RELATIONSHIP WITH GOD

Both Job and Paul had relationships with God. With Job, it was a relationship based on fearing God and keeping clean before His holiness and justice. He had heard of God but did not know Him intimately. Paul knew the Law and all he had been taught throughout his Jewish upbringing and studies. Paul, like Job, would have had a fear of God and known His justice and holiness. However, Paul's relationship with God, after his conversion, changed. He had a newfound Father/son relationship with God.[1] He knew deeply the grace message; it was the foundation of all Paul preached. Pleasing God no longer was measured by sacrifices and offerings. Now, it was through faith and by grace. He had the revelation, too of, GOD IS LOVE. This can be clearly seen in First Corinthians 13 and Second Corinthians 13:11, 14. In Second Corinthians 1:3 NIV, Paul even praises and names our Heavenly Father as "the God and Father of our Lord Jesus Christ, the Father of compassion and the God of all comfort." Why would Paul ever proclaim such a beautiful title of Him if He were One who did not take a thorn away when His child asked?

Once Job took the time to SEE God for Who He really is, Job's relationship with God changed as well. He could see that God loved him and, through that love, provided everything necessary for Job to live victoriously. Knowing this Love meant that Job no longer had to fear the wrath of God. He could trust Him for guidance and correction throughout his life and enjoy fellowship with his Creator. Job went from offering sacrifices in the off chance that someone had done something wrong to offering sacrifices at God's direction.[2]

UNDER ENEMY ATTACK

Both Job and Paul found themselves under attack from Satan. Job dealt with the enemy's attempts to rob, kill and destroy almost everything he had. Paul dealt with the "thorn in the flesh." Neither instance was from God. If there is any doubt, just make a column with "Steal/Kill/Destroy" on one side and "Life" on the other. In John 10:10 NKJV Jesus tells us, "The thief does not come except to steal, and to kill, and to destroy. I have come that they may have life, and that they may have it more abundantly." If a situation or circumstance falls in the first column, it originated from the enemy. If it falls under the heading of "Life," it comes from God. "For with You is the fountain of life; In Your light we see light" (Ps. 36:9 NKJV).

CALLING OUT TO GOD

Both men cried out to God. Job called out to seek an audience to plead his case to a Most Holy Judge. Job wanted answers as to why, when he did everything he could think of to remain pure, he was afflicted. Paul called out to his Father to get rid of the thorn for him. Job spent chapter after chapter calling out to God but really did not take the time to stop and listen for God's answer until the end of the book that carries his name. Paul, on the other hand, listened after seeking God three times. In the case of Acts 16, it appeared to be after a matter of days. It was then that he understood that God was giving Paul the opportunity to exercise his authority as a believer. The next chance Paul had to confront the thorn, he did. If Job had just been quicker to listen, I believe both his time of suffering and his book would have been much shorter!

A REFUGE AND A PLAN

For each man, God had a place of refuge and a plan for their good. For Job, God provided a hedge of protection. All Job needed to do was to abide there. For Paul, he, too, had the promises of Psalm 91. They both had a refuge found in God Himself. God had a plan and a purpose for both men. Thankfully, both men were able to get into the flow of the plans God had for their lives. Job was able to stand in a place as High Priest and advocate for his family and friends. Paul was able to continue as an apostle and spread the Gospel of Jesus not only to the people of his day but also throughout time since and times to come with his writings.

EQUIPPED

God fully furnished Job and Paul with what they needed in order to be overcomers. Today, we can rely on all the wonderful tools He has prepared for those who follow Him. There are endless resources for us including the Word of God, Holy Spirit, the Armor of God, the fruits and gifts of Holy Spirit, the Name of Jesus and the Blood of the Lamb. "All Scripture is given by inspiration of God, and is profitable for doctrine, for reproof, for correction, for instruction in righteousness, that the man of God may be <u>complete, thoroughly equipped for every good work</u>" (2 Tim. 3:16, 17 NKJV).

VICTORY

Both Job and Paul experienced victory over the attacks of the enemy. A most LOVING God furnished this victory. With so much compassion for his children, He made a way for us all to be victorious in Him.

---

1 See Gal. 4:5-7
2 See Job 42:8, 9

Chapter Forty

Relevance for Today

Whose Report to Believe

For far too long the struggles of Job and the thorn in the flesh have skewed people's view of the Father. It wasn't scripture's account of these instances that brought confusion. Instead, it was our "dear comforters" of experience, tradition and legalism. They have loudly proclaimed that God put Job and Paul through these intense times in order to make them humble, to teach them something, to make them bow to Him. Operating within many, these comforters have largely gone uncontested; convincing people of their narrative. In doing so, they have hindered people from fully receiving from God all He has for them. Countless times, I have endeavored to tell others how it is God's will for them to be healed, healthy and whole. Many times, in return, I have been questioned, "What about Job? What about Paul's thorn in the flesh?" I am still puzzled as to why people insist on arguing against the absolute goodness of God. One would think people would be overjoyed to know that God wants them well! It is my earnest hope that, with this book, the arguments related to Job and Paul will be repudiated and end. Looking through the lens of love, we have found out that God was not the source of Job and Paul's troubles. He, instead, was the source of their protection and victory.

SOME EXAMPLES

Notice in Numbers 33:55, whose job it was to drive out the inhabitants. It wasn't God's responsibility to drive them out. The Israelites were supposed to do it. The Israelites were to drive out the inhabitants and God would back them up when they did. If and when the Israelites would take the step of faith to do so, God would ensure their victory. Whenever the Israelites lacked wisdom or strength, God's grace would most certainly step in to accomplish the task.

Think, too, of Peter when he walked on water with Jesus.[1] Peter took a step of faith in stepping out of the comfortable boat. As a fisherman, the boat was a place he knew. Stepping out onto the water was an act of faith. The faith was lying dormant, inactivated so long as he sat in the boat merely believing he could walk on the water. His faith without action was dead.[2] As he acted on his faith and stepped out of the boat, he was able to walk on the water with Jesus! When he turned his attention away from Jesus and onto the wind and the waves, Matthew 14:30 says that Peter started to sink. He didn't immediately plummet to the bottom of the sea. He **started** to sink. It was in that moment when God's grace was sufficient for Peter! In Peter's weakness, he was made strong. He got his focus back on Jesus and Jesus got Peter back to the boat. Did Peter fail? No. He did not drown. Plus, he is the only man recorded in the Bible to walk on the water with Jesus.

It is the same with us today. When we have a situation arise, we are to use the tools given us by God and step out in faith to act. We cannot sit back and beg God to do for us what He has designed us to do and then blame Him when the circumstances go unchanged. He is waiting for us to take our place, gird up our loins and operate in the authority He bestowed upon us when we accepted Jesus as our Lord and Savior.

---

1 See Matt. 14:29
2 See James 2:17

Chapter Forty-One

Is your Lens in Focus? Challenge

It is my heartfelt desire that GOD IS LOVE will shine through the pages of this book. If the arguments people associate with Job and Paul can be silenced, people will no longer be hindered in seeing the truth of Who God really is and His desires toward His creation. Instead of listening to the voices of tradition, experience and legalism, let us strive to renew our mind by the Word of God.[1] Jesus is the Truth![2] Jesus is the Word![3] Let us renew our mind with the Word and find the Truth!

The following page is dedicated to scriptures showing God's love and His desire for you to be healthy and whole. Renew your mind with these scriptures. From this point on, whenever you hear or read anything concerning God, including in the Bible, put on the lens of love and hear/read it through that lens. If it doesn't seem to mesh, cast aside any traditional teaching you've heard on the matter and meditate on the scripture itself. Then allow Holy Spirit to show you Truth. It will always make sense as Holy Spirit reveals it to you in a new and living way

---

1 See Rom. 12:2
2 John 14:6
3 John 1:1, 14

SCRIPTURES

God's Lovingkindness
Ps. 17:7
Ps. 26:3
Ps. 36:7
Ps. 36:10
Ps. 42:8
Ps. 63:3
Ps. 89:33
Ps. 103:4
Ps. 107:43
Ps. 138:2
Ps. 143:8
Jer. 9: 24
Jer. 31:3
Hos. 2:19
Jonah 4:2

The Love of God/Love
Prov. 8:17
Song of Sol. 1:2
Song of Sol. 2:4
Is. 63:9
Hosea 11:4
Zeph. 3:17
Luke 11:42
John 13:34
John 14:21
John 14:23
John 15:9

John 15:10
John 15:12
John 15:13
John 17:26
Rom. 5:5
Rom. 5:8
Rom. 8:35
Rom. 8:38-39
1 Cor. 13:4-8, 13
2 Cor. 13:11, 14
Eph. 2:4-10
Eph. 3:14-19
Eph. 5:2
Eph. 5:25
2 Thess. 3:5
1 Tim. 1:14
Titus 3:3-7
1 John 2:5
1 John 3:1
1 John 3:16
1 John 4:7-12
1 John 4:16
1 John 4:19

Tender Mercies
Ps. 25:6
Ps. 119:156
Ps. 145:9

Prayers

A Prayer for Salvation

Almighty God, I come to you now knowing that I am unable to save myself. I recognize that I have sinned and am a sinner. I ask for Your forgiveness and receive Jesus, Your Son, Whom You raised from the dead, as my personal Saviour. I accept Jesus taking the death penalty meant for me upon Himself. I receive the gift of right-standing with You that Jesus paid the price in full for me to have. I thank you that I am no longer a sinner. I am now a new creation in Christ Jesus. I thank you for the fullness of salvation and that I am able to come boldly to Your throne of Grace. I pray that You will help me to develop a deep, personal relationship with You from this moment on. In Jesus' Name. Amen.

A Prayer for the Baptism in the Holy Spirit

Heavenly Father, now that I am Your child, I pray for Holy Spirit to baptize me, fill me, empower me and guide me. I receive my new prayer language by faith and thank you for it. In Jesus' Name. Amen.

A Prayer for Healing

Heavenly Father, I thank you that according to Isaiah 53:5 and First Peter 2:24, it is by the sufferings of Jesus that I have been healed. The provision for my healing was finished when Jesus was crucified. I receive my healing now by faith. I am not moved by symptoms or what my physical senses tell me. Instead, I stand fully on Your Word and Your promises. I thank You that You love me and want me well, healthy and whole. I receive it now in Jesus' Name. Amen.

Now to Him who is able to keep you from stumbling,
And to present *you* faultless
Before the presence of His glory with exceeding joy,
To God our Savior,
Who alone is wise,
Be glory and majesty,
Dominion and power,
Both now and forever.
Amen. (Jude 1: 24, 25 NKJV)

Manufactured by Amazon.ca
Bolton, ON